W9-BFY-030

Sports in America
1940–1949

SECOND EDITION

PHIL BARBER

SERIES FOREWORD BY
LARRY KEITH

CHELSEA HOUSE
PUBLISHERS
An imprint of Infobase Publishing

1940–1949, Second Edition
Sports in America

Copyright © 2010 Phil Barber
Foreword copyright © 2010 Larry Keith

Chelsea House
An imprint of Infobase Publishing
132 West 31st Street
New York NY 10001

Library of Congress Cataloging-in-Publication Data

Barber, Phil.
 Sports in America, 1940-1949 / Phil Barber. — 2nd ed.
  p. cm. — (Sports in America)
 Includes bibliographical references and index.
 ISBN-13: 978-1-60413-450-6 (hardcover : alk. paper)
 ISBN-10: 1-60413-450-X (hardcover : alk. paper) 1. Sports—United States—History—20th century. I. Title. II. Series.

 GV583.B34 2010
 796.0973'09044—dc22

                                              2009022570

Chelsea House books are available at special discounts when purchased in bulk quantities for businesses, associations, institutions, or sales promotions. Please call our Special Sales Department in New York at (212) 967-8800 or (800) 322-8755.

You can find Chelsea House on the World Wide Web at http://www.chelseahouse.com

Produced by the Shoreline Publishing Group LLC
President/Editorial Director: James Buckley Jr.
Contributing Editors: Jim Gigliotti, Beth Adelman
Text design by Thomas Carling, carlingdesign.com
Index by Nanette Cardon, IRIS
Cover printed by Bang Printing, Brainerd, Minn.
Book printed and bound by Bang Printing, Brainerd, Minn.
Date printed: July 2010

Photo credits: AP/Wide World: 9, 13, 14, 19, 20, 25, 31, 33, 35, 39, 40, 41, 43, 49, 55, 57, 59, 62, 65, 67, 70, 71, 73, 77, 83, 85, 89; Baseball Hall of Fame: 24, 28, 35 (inset), 39, 44, 58; Corbis: 7, 8, 11, 16, 21, 22, 27, 30, 46, 47, 52, 54, 61, 68, 69, 72, 75, 78, 80, 82, 87, 88; Getty Images: 37, 50, 53, 80; Shoreline Publishing Group: 64, 81. Sports icons by Bob Eckstein.

Printed in the United States of America.

10 9 8 7 6 5 4 3 2 1

This book is printed on acid-free paper.

CONTENTS

Jackie Robinson, baseball player and barrier breaker (page 66)

FOREWORD

BY LARRY KEITH

WHEN THE EDITORS OF SPORTS IN AMERICA invited me to write the foreword to this important historical series I recalled my experience in the 1980s as the adjunct professor for a new sports journalism course in the graduate school of Columbia University. Before granting their approval, the faculty at that prestigious Ivy League institution asked, Do sports matter? Are they relevant? Are they more than just fun and games?

The answer—an emphatic yes—is even more appropriate today than it was then. As an integral part of American society, sports provide insights to our history and culture and, for better or worse, help define who we are.

Sports In America is much more than a compilation of names, dates, and facts. Each volume chronicles accomplishments and expansions of the possible. Not just in the physical ability to perform, but in the ability to create goals and determine methods to achieve them. In this way, sports, the sweaty offspring of recreation and competition, resemble any other field of endeavor. I certainly wouldn't equate the race for a gold medal with the race to the moon, but the building blocks are the same: the intelligent application of talent, determination, research, practice, and hard work to a meaningful objective.

Sports matter because they show us in high definition. They communicate examples of determination, courage, and skill. They often embody a heroic human-interest story, overcoming poverty, injustice, injury, or disease. The phrase, "Sports is a microcosm of life," could also read "Life is a microcosm of sport."

Consider racial issues. When Jackie Robinson of the Brooklyn Dodgers broke through major league baseball's "color barrier" in 1947, the significance extended beyond the national pastime. Precisely because baseball was the national pastime, this epochal event reverberated throughout every part of American society.

To be sure, black stars from individual sports had preceded him (notably Joe Louis in boxing and Jesse Owens in track), and others would follow (Arthur Ashe in tennis and Tiger Woods in golf), but Robinson stood out as an important member of a team. He wasn't just playing with the Dodgers, he was traveling with them, living with them. He was a black member of a white athletic family. The benefits of integration could be appreciated far beyond the borough of Brooklyn. In 1997, Major League Baseball retired his "42" jersey number.

Sports have always been a laboratory for social awareness and change. Robinson integrated big league box scores eight years before the U.S. Supreme Court ordered the integration of public schools. The Paralympics (1960) and Special Olympics (1968) easily predate the Americans with Disabilities Act (1990). The mainstreaming of disabled athletes was especially apparent in 2007 when double amputee Jessica Long, 15, won the AAU Sullivan Award as America's top amateur. Women's official debut in the Olympic Games, though limited to swimming, occurred in 1912, seven years before they got the right to vote. So even if these sports were tardy in opening their doors, in another way, they were ahead of their times. And if it was necessary to break down some of those doors—Title IX support for female college athletes comes to mind—so be it. Basketball star Candace Parker won't let anyone keep her from the hoop.

Another area of importance, particularly as it affects young people, is substance abuse. High school, college, and professional teams all oppose the illegal use of drugs, tobacco, and alcohol. In most venues, testing is mandatory, and tolerance is zero. The confirmed use of performance enhancing drugs has damaged the reputations of such superstar athletes as Olympic sprinters Ben Johnson and Marion Jones, cyclist Floyd Landis, and baseball sluggers Manny Ramirez and Alex Rodriguez. Some athletes have lost their careers, or even their lives, to substance abuse. Conversely, other athletes have used their fame to caution young people about submitting to peer pressure or making poor choices.

Fans care about sports and sports personalities because they provide entertainment and self-identify—too often at a loss of priorities. One reason sports have flourished in this country is their support from governmental bodies. When a city council votes to help underwrite the cost of a sports facility or give financial advantages to the owners of a team, it affects the pocketbook of every taxpayer, not to mention the local ecosystem. When high schools and colleges allocate significant resources to athletics, administrators believe they are serving the greater good, but at what cost? Decisions with implications beyond the sports page merit everyone's attention.

In World War II, our country's sporting passion inspired President Franklin Roosevelt to declare that professional games should not be cancelled. He felt the benefits to the national psyche outweighed the risk of gathering large crowds at central locations. In 2001, another generation of Americans also continued to attend large-scale sports events because, to do otherwise, would "let the terrorists win." Being there, being a fan, yelling your lungs out, cheering victory and bemoaning defeat, is a cleansing, even therapeutic exercise. The security check at the gate is just part of the price of stepping inside. Even before there was a 9/11, there was a bloody terrorist assault at the Munich Olympic Games in 1972.

The popular notion "Sports build character" has been better expressed "Sports reveal character." We've witnessed too many coaches and athletes break rules of fair play and good conduct. The convictions of NBA referee Tim Donaghy for gambling and NFL quarterback Michael Vick for operating a dog-fighting ring are startling recent examples. We've even seen violence and cheating in youth sports, often by parents of a (supposed) future superstar. We've watched (at a safe distance) fans "celebrate" championships with destructive behavior. I would argue, however, that these flaws are the exception, not the rule, that the good of sports far outweighs the bad, that many of life's success stories took root on an athletic field.

Any serious examination of sports leads to the question of athletes as standards for conduct. Professional basketball star Charles Barkley created quite a stir in 1993 when he used a Nike shoe commercial to declare, "I am not paid to be a role model." The knee-jerk response argued, "Of course you are, because kids look up to you," but Barkley was right to raise the issue. He was saying that, in making lifestyle choices in language and behavior, young people should look elsewhere for role models, ideally to responsible parents or guardians.

The fact remains, however, that athletes occupy an exalted place in our society, especially when they are magnified in the mass media, sports talk radio, and the blogosphere. The athletes we venerate can be as young as a high school basketball player or as old as a Hall of Famer. (They can even be dead, as Babe Ruth's commercial longevity attests.) They are honored and coddled in a way few mortals are. Regrettably, we can be quick to excuse their excesses and ignore their indulgences. They influence the way we live and think: Ted Williams inspired patriotism as a wartime fighter pilot; Muhammad Ali's opposition to the Vietnam War on religious grounds, validated by the Supreme Court, encouraged the peace movement; Magic Johnson's contraction of the HIV/AIDs virus brought better understanding to a little-understood disease. No wonder we elect them—track stars, football coaches, baseball pitchers—to represent us in Washington. Meanwhile, television networks pay huge sums to sports leagues so their teams can pay fortunes for their services.

Indeed, it has always been this way. If we, as a nation, love sports, then we, quite naturally, will love the men and women who play them best. In return, they provide entertainment, release and inspiration. From the beginning of the 20th century until now, Sports In America is their story-and ours.

Larry Keith is the former Assistant Managing Editor of Sports Illustrated. *He created the editorial concept for* SI Kids *and was the editor of the official Olympic programs in 1996, 2000 and 2002. He is a former adjunct professor of Sports Journalism at Columbia University and is a member of the North Carolina Journalism Hall of Fame.*

INTRODUCTION
1940–1949

WHAT IS THE PLACE OF SPORTS within the greater society? Do the games exist merely to entertain, or can they have larger impacts on the world and its people? For decades, games and sports were seen by "serious" people as either distractions or as merely ways to build a healthy body. However, as the world emerged from a destructive war, sports, for perhaps the first time, helped to become a force for change and for good.

As the decade dawned, World War II gripped much of the world. By 1940, the United States was a behind-the-scenes participant, sending arms and equipment to allies that included Great Britain. But as the Axis powers—Germany, Japan, and Italy—gobbled up territory, it appeared inevitable that America would join the fight outright. The decision was cemented on December 7, 1941, when the Japanese bombed the U.S. Navy fleet at Pearl Harbor in Hawaii.

Soon many of America's best young men and women, and most of its natural resources, were headed for war. The Selective Service Act was passed in the fall of 1940, making it possible for the government to draft men into the armed forces, and within two years at least 31 million men had registered for the draft. More than half of them wound up serving, and inevitably, some were drawn from the sports world. Stars and nobodies, veterans and rookies, all of them mobilized. The National Football League (NFL) lost 638 of its players, coaches, and officials to the armed forces; 66 of them were decorated in battle and 21 died in combat, including 12 active players.

The casualties certainly weren't limited to the big team sports. Torger Tokle, a Norwegian immigrant who set an American ski jump record in 1941, then broke it twice more (topping out at 289 feet), died while fighting in the Italian mountains with a U.S. ski-patrol force in 1944.

Even the athletes who stayed in the United States made sacrifices. Sports equipment manufacturers set a tone for the era by urging their consumers to "use it up, wear it out, make do, or do without." With rubber in short supply, most tennis and golf balls manufactured during World

Day of Infamy *December 7, 1941: The USS* Arizona *blows up in Pearl Harbor during the Japanese attack.*

War II were made of a combination of reclaimed and crude rubber, or a synthetic alternative. Tennis players called the mushy balls they played with "victory balls." Golfers complained that an average drive of 225 yards shrunk to 210 with their new balls.

Along the way, some now-revered traditions were conceived. In baseball, for example, crowds started singing the National Anthem before every game, and they kept the tradition going even after the war ended. Major League Baseball also began to play more night games during the war, in part to accommodate factory workers. The Westinghouse Electric Company supported the idea by reporting that stadium lights would use less power than the desk lamps of individual fans reading at home.

1940−1949

The Japanese, huge baseball fans themselves, knew how important sports were to Americans. They tried to jam broadcasts of the World Series over the Armed Forces Radio Network, and U.S. soldiers reported their Japanese enemies shouted, "To hell with Babe Ruth!" as they stormed fortified positions.

Finally, in 1945, after nearly four years of intense fighting since the United States' official entry into the war, World War II came to an end. Americans celebrated by flocking to ballparks, stadiums, courts, and rinks. Life returned to normal. "Dreams of baseball were dreams of sanity," Arthur Daley wrote in *The New York Times* on April 14, 1946. "To the dreamers the game was a symbol of the things-that-were, of the things-yet-to-be."

America entered World War II in the throes of an economic depression. Now the economy was humming, ramped up by the war effort, and sports fans had money to spend. The 1945 World Series, played just one month after the Japanese surrendered, set records for attendance (333,457 people) and gate receipts (nearly $1.6 million). In 1946, the Indianapolis Speedway welcomed 175,000 people to the Indy 500 auto race, and basketball crowds at all professional and college levels totaled some 75 million. Clearly, Americans were ready for some recreation.

However, as events would prove, Americans were ready for change, too, and sports would lead the way. After being sources of joy and diversion during the war, baseball games soon became centers of a a vast societal change.

Specifically, African-Americans were demanding equality, and many whites were ready to back them up. As baseball commissioner Albert "Happy" Chandler said, "If they [blacks] can fight and die on Okinawa, Guadalcanal, in the South Pacific, they can play ball in America."

In 1946, two football teams in competing leagues—the National Football League's Los Angeles Rams and the All-America Football Conference's Cleveland Browns—suited up African-American players. It was a relatively quiet achievement for the Rams' Kenny Washington and Woody Strode and the Browns' Bill Willis and Marion Motley.

By contrast, when Jackie Robinson joined baseball's Brooklyn Dodgers a

Other Kinds of Uniforms *Yankees superstar Joe DiMaggio (left) and Dodgers sparkplug Pee Wee Reese (second from right) were among many athletes who joined the armed forces during the war.*

Lasting Impact *Jackie Robinson's life had a positive impact on many lives. This rose rests at his grave in 1997, 50 years after he shattered baseball's color barrier.*

year later, it was one of the biggest sports stories of the decade, or, some might say, of the century. Baseball was by far the most popular sport in the 1940s, and its color barrier had been silently enforced since the turn of the century. But Dodgers president Branch Rickey decided the time had come to shatter that barrier, and he chose Robinson to do it. The 1947 season tested Robinson's resolve, but by October he helped Brooklyn get to the World Series and was voted Rookie of the Year for both leagues. The game never looked back. The Cleveland Indians' Larry Doby integrated the American League in 1948, and many other teams soon followed suit.

If the 1940s brought growing pains to some of the established professional sports, they announced the birth of others. The National Basketball Association, NASCAR, the Ladies Professional Golf Association, and a legitimate professional tennis tour all arose in the second half of the decade.

Having survived the crucible of war and having begun to fight the battle for integration, American sports were ready for a golden age.

1940

War and Sports

The Olympic movement had been part of the international sports scene since 1896. In Japan, the year 1940 was supposed to be the year that that country finally made a big mark on the worldwide sports extravaganza. It was scheduled to be the host of the Olympics that year. The emerging country was scheduled to host both the Winter Olympics in Sapporo and the Summer Olympics in Tokyo.

By 1937, that plan had come undone. In 1931, the Japanese government invaded Manchuria in northern China. Japan attacked into the heart of China in 1937, beginning a war that would last seven years and spread throughout the Pacific. Not surprisingly, due to the conflict, Japan canceled its Olympics.

As alternatives, the International Olympic Committee (IOC) selected St. Moritz, Switzerland, for the Winter Games and Helsinki, Finland, for the Summer Games. However, plans there fell through, as did additonal plans to hold the Winter Games in Germany. Again, war cancelled those events, too.

Clearly, this was no time for international sports competitions. Unwillingly, the IOC canceled the Games for the first time in the modern era.

The 1944 Olympic Games, scheduled for London and Cortina d'Ampezzo, Italy, would be canceled as well.

The Flying Dutchman

Pole vaulting actually began as a contest of distance, not height. Vaulters would use poles to leap across wide canals or streams. However, by the time the Olympics began, using a pole to propel the athlete over a bar was the standard. Still, like a too-wide canal, a barrier remained: 15 feet.

Finally, Cornelius "Dutch" Warmerdam cleared that elusive height on April 13. Warmerdam, a 24-year-old high school teacher, was competing for the San Francisco Olympic Club at Berkeley, California.

Warmerdam's record-breaking vault measured 15 feet, 1 1/8 inches. This was no lucky leap. Competing at Fresno, California, on June 29, he bettered the mark by nearly two inches. And he continued to shatter his own record, inch by inch, until he hit 15 feet, 8 1/2 inches in 1943. "The Flying Dutchman" retired from the sport

Record Setter *Warmerdam's heroics made him a national sports icon.*

in 1944, having topped 15 feet an incredible 43 times.

Observers of the day swear no one has ever exhibited better form in the pole vault than Warmerdam. His vaults are far lower than those today, but Dutch made his vaults with a wooden pole. The modern fiberglass pole didn't come along until the 1960s, and soon after, men were vaulting more than 17 feet.

1940

One Tough Feller

The Cleveland Indians' hard-throwing pitcher, Bob Feller (b.1918), had been the class of the American League in 1939, leading the league in wins (24), innings pitched (296), and strikeouts (246). So everyone expected him to have a big season in 1940. They just didn't know how quickly he'd get rolling. Feller took the mound on April 16 and threw a no-hitter, blanking the Chicago White Sox 1–0. It is still the only Opening Day no-hitter in Major League Baseball history.

The 21-year-old Feller had an exceptional season. He won 27 games for the Indians, with 261 strikeouts in 320 innings and a league-leading earned run average (ERA) of 2.61. (ERA is a key measure of a pitcher's success; it shows how many earned runs a pitcher allows every nine innings.)

Yankees Go Home

The 1930s belonged to the New York Yankees. They won every World Series from 1936 through 1939, the first team to win four baseball championships in a row. In fact, they swept the Series in four straight games in both 1938 and 1939. In 1940, the team was once again great, led by outfielder Joe DiMaggio (1914–1999), but it didn't finish at the top.

This time, the Bronx Bombers fell short. In a tight, three-team race, it was the Detroit Tigers who beat the Cleveland Indians (by a game) and the Yankees (by two games) to take the pennant. The Tigers were powered by a couple of mighty sluggers: outfielder Hank Green-berg (1911–1986; a .340 batting average and 41 home runs in 1940) and first baseman Rudy York (33 homers and 134 RBI). Their best pitcher, Bobo Newsom, won 21 games and lost only five.

Pitching ruled the National League in 1940, and no team had better arms than the Cincinnati Reds. Their best was Bucky Walters, who led the league in wins (22) and innings pitched (305), and had a dazzling ERA of 2.48. The Reds were only average at the plate, but they had brilliant fielders to back up the pitchers.

The World Series in October went seven games, and was largely a contest between Walters and Newsom. Both were nearly invincible. Walters won two complete games, giving up only eight hits and three runs. Newsom won the first and fifth games, even though his father died after watching the victorious game one. Newsom valiantly pitched game seven on just one day of rest, and lost to Derringer as the Reds claimed their first championship in 21 years on October 8. For the Series, though, Newsom gave up a mere four runs in 26 innings.

Undaunted by his personal losses, the colorful Newsom arrived at spring training the following season in a car with a neon sign that read "Bobo" and a horn that played the popular song "Hold That Tiger."

Chicago Punts Football

The University of Chicago football team had plenty of success on the field. The school had, in fact, produced the nation's first Heisman Trophy winner, Jay Berwanger, in 1935. But in 1940, university President Robert Hutchins shocked the student body by announcing that the school was dropping its football program. "There is no doubt that football has been a major handicap to education in the United States," Hutchins said in an address. He noted with scorn that 50 percent of Big Ten football players were physical-education majors.

The president wrapped up his argument by stating, "I think it is a good thing for this country to have one important university discontinue football."

If Hutchins hoped for other colleges to follow suit, he was disappointed. But the University of Chicago still has no football team—preferring, instead, to churn out Nobel Prize winners.

T Time for Frankie

Few college football teams were more inept than the Stanford University Indians in 1939. The Indians finished 1–7–1, losing every Pacific Coast Conference game they played. But in 1940, Stanford benefited from the decision at Chicago (see page 12) and hired that university's former coach, the innovative Clark Shaughnessy. The coach had developed a T-formation offensive scheme, which sent men in motion before the ball was snapped and used many more passing plays than other formations, and it was about to take the football world by storm.

Stanford began the season in September against a pretty good University of San Francisco team and won easily, 27–0. The Indians proceeded to notch victories against the University of Oregon

(13–0), the University of Santa Clara (7–6), and Washington State University (26–14). Still, few thought Stanford could beat the University of Southern California (USC) on October 26. USC hadn't lost a game since 1938 and had beaten Stanford three times in a row.

Suited to the T *Stanford quarterback Frankie Albert's success with the T formation helped make it the standard for football teams.*

The Beginning of the End

Before 1935, NFL teams passed the ball only out of desperation, or as a form of trickery. Don Hutson (1913–1997) helped change that—not by throwing the ball, but by catching it better than anyone had before.

They called Hutson the Alabama Antelope. He was fast, with reliable hands and great moves. One of his favorite moves involved grabbing a goal post (the posts were on the goal line in those days) with one arm and spinning himself away from a defender.

During his 11-year career (1935–1945) with Green Bay, Hutson led the NFL in receiving eight times. In 1942 he caught 74 passes; the next highest total was a distant 27. In 1944 he scored 29 points on four touchdowns while also kicking five extra points (after touchdowns) in a single quarter. He retired with 99 touchdowns—an NFL record that stood for 44 years.

Hutson became the first receiver to regularly see double coverage (where two defenders cover a single offensive player). And even that usually wasn't enough. "I just concede him two touchdowns a game and hope we can score more," Chicago Bears owner George Halas (1895–1983) said.

The Gipper   *Future president Ronald Reagan starred in a 1940 football movie.*

With three minutes to go, the game was tied 7–7. Then, quarterback Frankie Albert started faking handoffs and turning them into play-action passes (passes made after pretending to hand off the ball). This was the strength of the T, and no one had ever handled the ball better than Albert. He drove the Indians 80 yards for the go-ahead touchdown, then intercepted a USC pass with a little over a minute left and returned it for another score. Stanford won 21–7.

Powered by Albert, fullback Norm Standlee, and slashing halfback Pete Kmetovic, the Indians finished the regular season 10–0 and wrapped up a magical season by defeating the University of Nebraska 21–13 in the Rose Bowl on January 1. Within five years, most football teams in America—at every level of play—were using the T formation.

A Movie Legend

 The University of Notre Dame was one of the most successful and popular college football programs in the nation in this era. Part of the reason, of course, was its enormous success, as the school won national titles and dozens of games. However, in 1940, Notre Dame got a big boost from a Hollywood movie . . . and a young actor played a part that would make him famous.

The movie, called *Knute Rockne: All-American,* was mostly about the great coach of the "Fighting Irish." But the part of Notre Dame player George Gipp was played by actor Ronald Reagan. The part called for Reagan to perform on the football field, showing off his athletic skills. Gipp was fated to die, however, giving the actor a famous death scene. Pat O'Brien, playing Rockne, then gave his famous "Win One for the Gipper" speech that has become a regular part of American sports legend. Supposedly, several years after Gipp died, Rockne did indeed encourage his team, behind at halftime, to come back and win in memory of the fallen player.

Decades later, when Reagan was running for president, the role came to identify him. He was known as "The Gipper" during his campaign and presidency. The combination of the famous school, a legendary scene, and the president of the United States combined to make a man who played only two seasons of college football one of the most famous collegians of all time.

The Prime of Old 98

At the turn of the decade, few athletes could bring a crowd to its feet like Tommy Harmon (1919–1990), the University of Michigan's do-everything football halfback. "Old 98"—a reference to Harmon's jersey number—played offense and defense for the Wolverines. He was a productive passer and a sensational open-field runner who shredded defenses in 1939 and 1940, winning the Heisman Trophy as a senior. In a win over the University of California at Berkeley in 1940, he scored on sensational runs of 94, 72, 86, and 80 yards. He also scored three touchdowns and passed for another in the Wolverines' 40–0 rout of rival Ohio State.

After college, Harmon signed with the New York Americans of the American Football League, a short-lived rival to the NFL. He later played two seasons (1946–47) for the Los Angeles Rams. That was

Justice on the Field

The NFL's leading rusher in 1940 was a man who would gain more acclaim in a black robe than he ever did in a football jersey. He was Byron "Whizzer" White (b.1917), who went on to a 31-year tenure as a U.S. Supreme Court Justice, after being appointed by President John F. Kennedy in 1962.

White, a celebrated student-athlete at the University of Colorado, first led the professional league's rushers as a rookie with the Pittsburgh Pirates in 1938. He then spent a year at Oxford University in Britain, studying on a Rhodes scholarship. He returned to play for the Detroit Lions in 1940 and used his shifty moves to rush for 514 yards. After one more season, he left football and turned his attention to larger matters. His rise to legal fame didn't surprise any of his teammates.

As Lions coach George Clark once said, "While the other guys were playing cards for five cents a point, White would get out his glasses, his pipe, and his law books and start studying."

1940

after being a fighter pilot in World War II, which would leave him with a Silver Star, a Purple Heart, and an injured leg. He just wouldn't be the runner who had thrilled fans at the collegiate level.

Asked to compare some of the great backs he had seen over his long and decorated career, famed coach Amos Alonzo

Super Sid   *Chicago quarterback Sid Luckman led a 1940 title-game rout that set a standard for high scoring.*

Stagg (1862–1965) said, "I'll take Harmon on my team, and you can have the rest."

73–0!

The NFL's fiercest rivalry of the era pitted the Chicago Bears against the Washington Redskins. They played for the league championship in 1937, and again in 1942 and 1943. Each team had a great passer, Washington's Sammy Baugh (1914–2008) and Chicago's Sid Luckman (1916–1998). Most important, the two team owners—George Halas of the Bears and George Preston Marshall of the Redskins—were proud and fiery men who basically couldn't stand one another.

After Washington edged Chicago 7–3 on November 17, Halas and his players angrily complained about a controversial call made in the final seconds. Marshall responded by labeling the Bears "a bunch of crybabies."

With the Redskins winning the Eastern Division on the strength of a 9–2 record and the Bears capturing the Western Division at 8–3, the stage was set for a rematch. Halas, the head coach as well as the owner, fumed about Marshall's remark as the game approached. He also recruited Stanford University coach Clark Shaughnessy (see page 13), who tinkered with the offense in the days leading up to the grudge match on December 8.

The Redskins didn't know what hit them. Fifty-five seconds into the game, Bears fullback Bill Osmanski took a handoff and blazed down the left sideline. End George Wilson blasted two defenders out of the way, and Osmanski was gone for a 68-yard touchdown. The next time they got the ball, Luckman drove the Bears 80 yards and scored on a quarterback sneak. On the first play of the next possession, fullback Joe Maniaci raced 42 yards for a touchdown. It was 21–0 at the end of the first quarter, 28–0 at halftime, and it only got worse in the second half.

This was the first pro football game to be broadcast over an entire radio network—120 stations via the Mutual Broadcasting System, which paid $2,500 for the rights—and the announcer, the legendary Red Barber (1908–1992), couldn't believe what he was seeing. "The touchdowns came so quickly there for awhile, I felt like I was the cashier at a grocery store," Barber said. "It is a very good thing I went over the roster of the Bears. I believe I wound up having to say every player's name on the list. In fact, I believe they all scored touchdowns."

Indeed, 10 different Bears took the ball into the end zone. And Luckman didn't even play in the second half. Halas pulled many of his starters as the margin grew. When the score reached 67–0, the public address announcer at Griffith Stadium bravely reminded Redskins fans that it was never too early to order tickets for 1941. He was drowned out by boos.

By late in the game, footballs were scarce because so many extra-point kicks had landed in the stands. So the officials ordered the Bears to run or pass for their conversions. They missed four extra points in all, detracting only a bit from the dizzying final score of 73–0. The NFL has never had a bigger blowout, before or since.

In all, Chicago rushed for 381 yards, completed 7 of 10 passes for another 138 yards, and intercepted eight passes.

Other Milestones of 1940

✔ On February 28, WXBS (later WNBC) televised the first college basketball games. The broadcast was a doubleheader: University of Pittsburgh versus Fordham University and New York University versus Georgetown, at New York's Madison Square Garden.

✔ The University of Illinois won the first intercollegiate gymnastics team championship on May 11.

✔ Basketball's Harlem Globetrotters defeated the Chicago Bruins to claim the World Championship Tournament. The Bruins' owner was George Halas, who ran the NFL's Chicago Bears.

✔ Belle Martel of Van Nuys, California, became the first female boxing referee when she presided over eight fights in San Bernardino.

Washington replaced Baugh with Frank Filchock, but it hardly mattered. As Bears tackle George Musso said, "It was the perfect football game. You can't play better than we did that day."

Marshall was predictably upset after the game. He told reporters his defense looked like "a roomful of maidens [young women] going after a mouse," and that his offense wasn't much better.

It was a dark day in the nation's capital, where politicians and generals already worried about the German bombing of London and the occupation of Paris. But in Chicago, for one day at least, there was pure joy.

1941

Whirlaway Crowned

On May 3, jockey Eddie Arcaro (1916–1997) rode the horse Whirlaway to a record time of 2:01 2/5 in the Kentucky Derby. A week later the duo claimed the Preakness Stakes. The Belmont Stakes was nearly a month later, on June 7, and more than 30,000 racing fans turned out to see whether Arcaro and Whirlaway could win racing's coveted Triple Crown.

Whirlaway was a spirited chestnut colt, the son of Blenheim II and Dustwhirl. He was bred on Calumet Farms, the country's premier Thoroughbred breeder. Calumet's owner, Warren Wright, missed the Belmont to attend his son's graduation ceremony, but insiders figured his absence was because he just wasn't worried about the race. His horse, after all, was a heavy 1-to-4 favorite.

Arcaro's usual strategy aboard the tireless Whirlaway was to hang back until the final stretch. "But at the mile post, there was no pace," he explained later. "It was very slow. So I yelled to those other jocks, 'I'm leaving.'"

And so he was. Whirlaway bolted to the front of the pack before the half-mile

mark (the race was a mile and a half) and won by three lengths, making Whirlaway the fifth horse to capture the Triple Crown. Arcaro never had to use the whip in this one.

Conn's Folly

Joe Louis was making a mockery of boxing's heavyweight division, defeating all challengers and making it look easy. When former light-heavyweight champion Billy Conn, a tough Irish-American from Pittsburgh, moved up to take a shot at Louis, nobody gave him

On the Way to 56 *With this swing, Joe DiMaggio advanced his hitting streak to 39 consecutive games (page 20).*

much of a chance. In fact, the only person who seemed to take Conn seriously was Conn himself. "He won't get away from me when he's hurt," the brash 25-year-old told reporters, referring to Louis.

The two boxers met at the Polo Grounds in Manhattan on June 18. Promoters set up wooden chairs on the New York Giants' baseball field, and the 54,487 in attendance included many uniformed soldiers and sailors. Just about everyone expected Conn, who was 25 pounds lighter, to dance away from Louis in an attempt to tire him out. But he charged right at the champion and shocked the crowd with his effectiveness. It was an action-packed fight. Conn was cut on the bridge of his nose and over his right eye in the fifth round, while Louis got a bloody nose in the ninth round.

By the 12th round, it was clear that Conn had out-boxed Louis. Most observers agreed that all he had to do was avoid the big man's right cross for three more rounds, and Conn would be the new heavyweight champion.

Conn on the Canvas *Joe Louis heads for a neutral corner while the referee moves in for the count after Louis decked challenger Billy Conn in their June heavyweight fight, which Conn almost won.*

56 for 56

Throughout the decades, baseball has generated millions of numbers. Statistics such as batting average, number of home runs, total strikeouts, and more let fans compare the players from different eras. Some of those numbers became so well-known that they described in mere digits incredible feats. For instance, just say the number "56" to a longtime baseball fan and you'll get only one answer: Joe DiMaggio. In 1941, DiMaggio got at least one hit in that many games in a row. It was a streak that went 15 games past any other before him, and no one has come inside of a dozen games since.

The Streak began on May 15. DiMaggio got a single in four at-bats against the Chicago White Sox. Then the center fielder got hits in his next game, and the next. DiMaggio stretched it to 20 straight games on June 3 and to 25 games on June 10. Soon the entire nation was checking his performance in the morning papers and getting radio bulletins on every at-bat. Fans flocked to his games. Official scorers admitted to feeling the pressure (they didn't want to end or prolong the streak on a questionable play), but the unflappable DiMaggio never changed expression.

On June 28 he got a single and a double against the Philadelphia A's, tying George Sisler's (1893–1973) major-league mark of 41 consecutive games with a hit. DiMaggio broke the record the next day, singling against the Washington Senators. He made it to 50 games on July 11, pounding a home run and three singles against the St. Louis Browns.

Louis knew it, too, so he came out swinging in the 13th round. Instead of covering up and moving away, Conn decided to trade punches with the champion. It was a brave but foolhardy tactic.

Louis stunned Conn with a thunderous right to the jaw, then launched a left-right combination that knocked the challenger flat. The referee counted out Conn with only two seconds left in the round, and Louis remained heavyweight champion.

After the fight, the two boxers were mutually respectful. "Joe, you should've let me win that fight. Think of all the money we could make on the return," Conn said with a smile.

"I loaned you my title for 12 rounds," Louis replied, "and you couldn't keep it."

It all came to an end on July 17, before 67,468 people in Cleveland (to that point, the largest crowd ever to see a night baseball game), but Joltin' Joe DiMaggio didn't go quietly. In two of his first three at-bats against Indians pitcher Al Smith, he ripped the ball down the third base line. Each time, the Indians' Ken Keltner made a superb stop and threw across the field for the out.

Smith walked DiMaggio in his second at-bat. When DiMaggio came to bat in the eighth inning, right-handed knuckleball pitcher Jim Bagby was on the mound and the bases were loaded. The crowd was on pins and needles. The Yankees' star hit a bouncing ball to deep shortstop, where Cleveland player-manager Lou Boudreau turned it into a double play.

DiMaggio nearly got another chance. The Indians went into the bottom of the ninth trailing 4–1. But they scored twice and placed a man on third base with no outs. Had they gotten him home, DiMaggio was due to bat in the 10th inning. But base-running blunders sealed a 4–3 New York victory, and the end of the hitting streak at 56 games.

Amazingly, DiMaggio got a hit in the next game and began another streak of 16 games. His 56-game streak remains one of baseball's most most memorable and enduring feats.

The Hitting Machine

 During his sensational 56-game hitting streak, Joe DiMaggio batted for

Mr. Triple Crown

Jockey Eddie Arcaro was known as "The Master," and it wasn't just because he won so often—although winning was certainly part of the legacy. (He won 4,779 races in his career, including five Kentuckys Derby, six Belmont Stakes, and six Preakness Stakes.) What truly defined Arcaro were his quiet confidence in the saddle and his devotion to his profession.

George Edward Arcaro was born in Cincinnati, Ohio, in 1916. By the time he retired from racing in 1962, *Sports Illustrated* called him "the most famous

Eddie Arcaro

man to ride a horse since Paul Revere." He won the Triple Crown atop Whirlaway in 1941 and with Citation in 1948, and he barely missed with Nashua in 1955, finishing a close second in the Derby. Arcaro had an uncanny knack for avoiding bad position on the track, and he was one of the first jockeys to switch the whip from hand to hand.

After retiring, Arcaro was founder and first president of the Jockeys Guild, which provided health insurance and employment benefits to the long-overlooked riders.

Joltin' Joe

Joe DiMaggio

Someone once asked Joe DiMaggio why he played so hard day in and day out. He replied, "There might be someone in the park who's never seen me play before."

Or there might not be. Between 1936 and 1951, sports fans of all stripes (and especially pinstripes) filled ballparks to see the man they called the Yankee Clipper.

DiMaggio couldn't hit the ball as far as his Yankees' predecessor, Babe Ruth (1895–1948), or the slugger who followed him to Yankees' fame, Mickey Mantle (1931–1995). But he could do it all. He hit home runs (361), he hit for average (.325), and he ranged around center field like a gazelle. With his long stride and fluid grace, he made it all look easy. And while his reserved, private nature might today be viewed as aloofness, in the 1940s DiMaggio was considered the epitome of class. It didn't hurt that he played for the dominant team of the era, in the country's biggest media market.

Raised in San Francisco, the son of a fisherman, DiMaggio preceded two brothers—Vince and Dom—in the big leagues. Dom was a noted player in his own right. But it was Joe who inspired songs and poems and married America's biggest movie star, Marilyn Monroe, in 1954. And it's Joe who has come to symbolize the beauty and grace of sports in a purer time.

a robust .408 average. During that same span, the Boston Red Sox's Ted Williams (1918–2002) actually outdid Joltin' Joe, hitting. 410. When DiMaggio's streak ended, fans across the nation swiftly took notice of Williams.

As noted with DiMaggio and the number 56, baseball fans worship numerals. In talking of batting skill, the benchmark is .400. That is, a player averaging a hit four times out of every 10 at-bats. With a .300 average marking a player as a star, .400 puts him into a rare stratosphere. In fact, it has become nearly unattainable. When Williams came into his third pro season in 1941, no American Leaguer had hit .400

since 1923, when Harry Heilmann of the Detroit Tigers led the league at .403. Now Williams was making a serious run at the mark. As August turned to September, his average stood at .413. Then he went cold.

On the last day of the season, September 28, with a doubleheader to play, Williams was batting .39955. His manager, Joe Cronin (1906–1984), who was doubly busy hitting .311 as the Red Sox's shortstop, knew that the league would round up Williams' average to an even .400. With Boston far behind the Yankees in the standings, Cronin suggested the slugger take the day off and preserve his mark. Williams refused.

In the first game of the doubleheader he had four hits, including a home run. He got two more hits in the second game. All in all, he went six for eight and raised his average to a sparkling .406.

The average was only part of a phenomenal season for Williams. He led the league with 37 home runs, 145 walks, and 135 runs scored. Perhaps most impressive, he struck out only 27 times. It has been nearly 70 years since Williams hit .400. No one has done it since. The player who once set as a life goal to be the "best hitter who ever lived" had made a pretty good case that he was just that.

Go-Go Gophers

The Big Ten Conference was the seat of power in college football before World War II. And from 1933 through 1941, the dominant Big Ten team was Bernie Bierman's University of Minnesota Gophers. Minnesota's apex came in 1940 and 1941, when the team went undefeated over the course of the two seasons (16–0) and claimed back-to-back national championships.

Not that the victories always came easily. In 1940 Minnesota had narrowly beaten star halfback Tommy Harmon and the University of Michigan, winning 7–6. In 1941 the Gophers trailed Northwestern University 7–2 and seemed headed for defeat. But they called a play without a signal, caught Northwestern sleeping, and scored on a long touchdown run by Brad Higgins.

Halfback Bruce Smith, the pride of the 1941 Minnesota squad, won the Heisman Trophy.

The NFL's New Horseman

Since its start in 1920, the NFL had an elected president. But he had little power when it came to setting policy and punishing rule-breakers. NFL owners looked at baseball and its iron-fisted commissioner, Judge Kenesaw Mountain Landis (1866–1944), and decided they wanted similar leadership. Landis helped baseball rebound from the 1919 Black Sox World Series gambling scandal. His authority had organized the sport's often-bickering owners.

The NFL owners sought someone with a solid reputation and a recogniz-

Fantasy Football

Sports has a long history of creative pranks and spoofs. One popped up in 1941 and made John Chung one of America's most talked-about athletes. One problem: Chung did not exist. In the fall of 1941, reports were made about Plainfield Teachers College, which piled up a number of lopsided victories behind John Chung, a sophomore halfback from China.

However, the school was actually the creation of Morris Newburger, a Wall Street stockbroker with a little too much time on his hands. Posing as public-relations director Jerry Croyden, Newburger began calling *The New York Times* with scores and other details of Plainfield Teachers College games. Without checking up on "Croyden," *The Times* printed the results, and other newspapers followed.

On November 13, Newburger issued a press release stating, sadly, that Chung and his teammates had flunked their midterm exams and would play no more games. Four days later, *Time* magazine revealed the hoax.

1941

able name to do something similar. Their choice was Elmer Layden, who had been one of the famed Four Horsemen of the University of Notre Dame's Fighting Irish football team in 1924. Layden was now coaching the Fighting Irish and serving as the school's athletic director. He was just starting a new contract at the university, but the NFL brass convinced him to accept their offer to be the league's commissioner.

Carl L. Storck had been an NFL leader since 1920 and its acting president since 1939. He wasn't thrilled about acquiring a new boss in Layden. So Storck resigned from the job.

One Strike Away

A Winning Ticket *A fan with this ticket watched the Dodgers beat the Yankees.*

The 1941 World Series matchup was half-familiar to sports fans. The American League representative, Joe McCarthy's (1887–1978) New York Yankees, were making their fifth appearance in six years. But the National Leaguers, Leo Durocher's (1905–1991) Brooklyn Dodgers, hadn't been in the Series since 1920.

The subway rivals — Brooklyn is one of New York's five boroughs, as is the Yankees' home in the Bronx — were evenly matched, and the first three October games were decided by one run each. The Yankees took the first game 3–2, the Dodgers claimed game two by the same score, and New York scored twice in the eighth inning against Brooklyn relief ace Hugh Casey to win the third game 2–1.

Game four, played in Ebbets Field, Brooklyn, is one that lingers in the memory of New York sports fans. Through eight innings of another tense battle, Brooklyn clung to a 4–3 lead. Casey had taken the mound again, and he promptly retired the first two Yankees (Johnny Sturm and Red Rolfe) in the ninth inning. With three balls and two strikes on New York's Tommy Henrich, the crowd stood in anticipation of a victory by the hometown Dodgers. Brooklyn catcher Mickey Owen signaled for a curveball. Of course, he wasn't sure if Casey would be throwing his sharp-breaking curve or his big looper. The pitch fooled the batter completely. Henrich, a New York outfielder, swung and missed, and umpire Larry Goetz signaled a strikeout.

Unfortunately, the pitch fooled Owen as well. The ball glanced off his mitt and shot back to the wall. If a pitch gets past the catcher on a third strike, the batter is allowed to run to first base — and that's just what Henrich did. The next man up, Joe DiMaggio, singled to left. Casey was coming undone. Before the inning was over he yielded two-run doubles to both Charlie Keller and Joe Gordon. The Yankees won 7–4 and then trampled the Dodgers 3–1 in game five to win the title.

The War Comes to America

Though World War II had already cancelled the Winter and Summer Olympics (see page 10), its effects had not been really felt in the American sports world. Some players were choosing to enlist in the armed forces, but not enough to truly affect rosters.

Other Milestones of 1941

✔ The Amateur Athletic Union adopted synchronized swimming (an artistic swimming routine) as a sanctioned sport for doubles and team events. The first championship meet was held in Wilmette, Illinois, on March 1.

✔ Chicago and Green Bay tied atop the West Division and met in the first NFL divisional playoff December 14. Chicago won 33–14, then beat the New York Giants 37–9 for the league title.

NFL-champion Chicago Bears

✔ The National Collegiate Athletic Association (NCAA) basketball tournament final was broadcast nationally for the first time, by the Mutual Broadcasting Network. The University of Wisconsin defeated Washington State University, 39–34.

✔ The NFL spurned Spalding and adopted the Wilson football as its official ball. The move helped differentiate the professional game from college football.

However, a military draft was begun in 1940 and would call for hundreds of pro athletes, most from Major League Baseball, to put down their gloves and take up arms for Uncle Sam.

The first regular big-league player to get the call was Hugh Mulcahy, a pitcher for the Philadelphia Phillies. Mulcahy, drafted in March of 1941, missed almost five full seasons. By the end of 1941, 328 of 607 major leaguers were in the military.

The involvement of athletes—and Americans from all other walks of life—spiraled upward after December 7. This was the morning Japanese planes attacked the U.S. naval base at Pearl Harbor, on the Hawaiian island of Oahu.

Because December 7 was a Sunday, several NFL games were in progress across the country. At the Polo Grounds in New York and at Comiskey Park in Chicago, public-address announcers interrupted their patter and directed all servicemen to report to their units. At Griffith Stadium in Washington, D.C., the announcer paged high-ranking government and military officials, but he did not mention the attack. For the fans in attendance, as well as the officials and servicemen called from their seats, this was the first time they had heard the news about the terrible attack and its effects.

The next day, America officially declared war against the Axis powers of Japan, Germany, and Italy. The war's impact on the world would be enormous. In the next few chapters, we'll see often how it touched the world of sports, too.

1942

What a Comeback!

For the Detroit Red Wings, it was the tale of two seasons. They finished fifth in the National Hockey League standings, but in a small league, they still made the playoffs. That was when they seemed to have found some magic potion. They were almost unstoppable.

Against all the odds, they made it to the Stanley Cup Finals. There they took on the Toronto Maple Leafs. The Leafs were loaded, with stars such as goalie Turk Broda and the great Syl Apps. No matter. The Red Wings kept rolling and won the first three games of the seven-game finals. Then the Red Wings seemed to return to regular-season form.

Playing before 13,694 crazed fans in Detroit in game four, the Maple Leafs were indeed on thin ice. The series looked to be over when the Red Wings went up 2–0 in the first period. Then Toronto regained its composure, fighting back to tie the game at 2–2 in the second period. Early in the third period, Detroit's Carl Lipscombe drilled a 35–foot slapshot that fooled Broda and put the home team up 3–2. It was Apps who bailed out the Maple Leafs this time, sneaking in front of the net and flicking in the puck to tie it at 3–3.

A pair of siblings finally put Toronto on top. Don Metz passed to Nick Metz, who threaded a shot for a 4–3 lead.

The Red Wings went after Broda with a vengeance, but referee Mel Harris whistled them for four penalties in the waning minutes of the game. They couldn't make up the gap shorthanded (in hockey, when a player takes a penalty his team plays a man short). After the game ended, Detroit coach Jack Adams and his players charged Harris to argue. A brawl ensued, leading to Adams' suspension.

Heartened by the win, Toronto came back to tie the series on consecutive shutouts by Broda. The Red Wings grabbed a 1–0 lead in game seven, in front of a then-record crowd at Maple Leaf Garden. But resilient Toronto again came back, relying on two goals by Sweeney Schriner to win 3–1 and earn its first Stanley Cup in a decade. The Maple Leafs were the only NHL team of the 20th century to come back from a 3–0 deficit in the finals.

(In 1945, the two teams tangled for the title again. This time, Toronto spurted to a three-game lead, only to see Detroit storm back to tie it. The Maple Leafs avoided a reversal of fortune by winning another game seven.)

Comeback Kings   *The 1942 Maple Leafs, seen here against the New York Rangers, won the Stanley Cup.*

Troubled Times

As battles raged on Midway Island in the Pacific and in North Africa, among other hot spots in World War II, the American public looked to sporting events for a sense of normalcy. But geopolitics and sports quickly started to mix.

In fact, the first day of the new year brought a shocking development. With Japanese submarines supposedly lurking in the Pacific, the U.S. government instituted an evening blackout for the West Coast. As a result, the Rose Bowl—the most prestigious college football bowl game—was moved to Durham, North Carolina. Despite its home-field advantage, on January 1, Duke University fell to Oregon State University, 20–16.

Other sports were also disrupted. Neither the Indianapolis 500 auto race nor the U.S. Open golf tournament was held

January 15, 1942.

My dear Judge:-

      Thank you for yours of January fourteenth. As you will, of course, realize the final decision about the baseball season must rest with you and the Baseball Club owners -- so what I am going to say is solely a personal and not an official point of view.

      I honestly feel that it would be best for the country to keep baseball going. There will be fewer people unemployed and everybody will work longer hours and harder than ever before.

      And that means that they ought to have a chance for recreation and for taking their minds off their work even more than before.

      Baseball provides a recreation which does not last over two hours or two hours and a half, and which can be got for very little cost. And, incidentally, I hope that night games can be extended because it gives an opportunity to the day shift to see a game occasionally.

      As to the players themselves, I know you agree with me that individual players who are of active military or naval age should go, without question, into the services. Even if the actual quality of the teams is lowered by the greater use of older players, this will not dampen the popularity of the sport. Of course, if any individual has some particular aptitude in a trade or profession, he ought to serve the Government. That, however, is a matter which I know you can handle with complete justice.

      Here is another way of looking at it -- if 300 teams use 5,000 or 6,000 players, these players are a definite recreational asset to at least 20,000,000 of their fellow citizens -- and that in my judgment is thoroughly worthwhile.

      With every best wish,

          Very sincerely yours,

Hon. Kenesaw M. Landis,   *Franklin D. Roosevelt*
333 North Michigan Avenue,
Chicago,
Illinois.

"Green Light Letter" *This letter from President Franklin Delano Roosevelt to Commissioner Landis gave Major League Baseball the "green light" to keep playing during the war years.*

in 1942, nor would they be for the next three years. In the NFL, Chicago Bears owner George Halas left for the Navy on November 1, and his backup quarterback, Young Bussey, departed about the same time. Halas returned in 1945; Bussey died in action.

In Major League Baseball, stars such as the Detroit Tigers' Hank Greenberg and the Cleveland Indians' Bob Feller joined the military. (Feller's Navy enlistment, two days after Pearl Harbor on December 9, 1941, was broadcast live on the radio.) Some older athletes who were not eligible for the draft enlisted nonetheless, lending their names to the war effort. Charlie Gehringer, who had played 19 fine seasons with Detroit, joined the Navy at the age of 39. He ran a physical-fitness program and rose to the rank of lieutenant commander. Ted Lyons, the Chicago White Sox's top pitcher for most of his 20 seasons, enlisted in the Marines at age 42.

Play Ball!

In 1942, Americans had a lot more on their mind than baseball. World War II was raging in Europe and Asia. Millions of American families were affected as loved ones entered the service . . . and in many cases did not come home. Amid all this, Major League Baseball commissioner Kenesaw Mountain Landis contacted President Franklin D. Roosevelt and offered to suspend baseball if the president felt that that would suit the needs of the country and the war effort. (In 1918, President Woodrow Wilson had halted all "nonessential industries" near the end of World War I, cutting short the 1918 baseball season, although the World Series had gone on that year and no seasons were canceled.)

Roosevelt's reply to Landis is remembered as the "Green Light Letter." It read, in part:

"I honestly feel that it would be best for the country to try to keep baseball going. There will be fewer people unemployed and everybody will work longer hours and harder than ever before. And that means that they ought to have a chance for recreation and for taking their minds off their work even more than before. . . . Here is another way of looking at it—if 300 teams use 5,000 or 6,000 players, these players are a definite recreational asset to at least 20,000,000 of their fellow citizens—and that in my judgment is thoroughly worthwhile."

Flight of the Cardinals

The St. Louis Cardinals' narrow misses were becoming all too familiar in baseball, having finished second in the National League in 1939 and 1941, and third in 1940. They seemed to take a step backward in 1942, but suddenly caught fire in mid-August and finished two games ahead of the second-place Brooklyn Dodgers.

The Cardinals didn't have a lot of pop; they hit only 60 home runs as a team. But their pitching was virtually flawless, led by Mort Cooper (22–7, 10 shutouts, 1.78 ERA) and Johnny Beazley (21–6, 2.13 ERA). As a staff, St. Louis' pitchers posted a stunning ERA of 2.55. Perhaps more important, the team was managed expertly by Billy Southworth, who regularly used 13 position players and eight pitchers .

In the American League, the New York Yankees' pitching staff of Red Ruffing, Spud Chandler, Ernie Bonham, and Hank Borowy was nearly as proficient as the Cardinals'. When the two teams met in the World Series in October, most fans expected a pitching duel.

Ruffing dominated game one, taking a no-hitter into the bottom of the eighth inning. He got his record seventh Series win, but the Cardinals' four runs

in the bottom of the ninth were an omen. St. Louis took the next four games, all of them close. Outfielder Enos Slaughter scored the winning run in game two, then third baseman Whitey Kurowski's two-run homer for St. Louis struck the final blow in the ninth inning of game five. The Cardinals were—finally—World Series champions.

The Home Front *The cover of the 1942 World Series program featured a young boy buying war stamps, sales of which went to aid the U.S. military during World War II.*

The Splendid Splinter *Ted Williams had nearly as many nick-names as he had clutch hits. He was known at various times as Teddy Ballgame, The Kid, and the Splendid Splinter, the latter a play on his skills with a wood bat and his lean frame.*

Teddy Ballgame

He was an average fielder and not much of a baserunner. But as a pure hitter, well, he was really something to see. Ted Williams, the Boston Red Sox's "Splendid Splinter," was the self-proclaimed "greatest hitter who ever lived."

In 1942 Williams had one his finest seasons. He won the American League Triple Crown, batting .356 with 36 home runs and 137 RBI, leading the league in all three batting categories.

His success came as a surprise to some who rememberd him as a high school senior in San Diego, California. In those days, Williams stood 6-foot-3 and weighed just 145 pounds. A Detroit Tigers' scout told Williams' mother that her son would probably die if he tried the major leagues. Fortunately for baseball fans in the 1940s and 1950s, Williams gained 60 pounds and developed into a menacing presence at the plate.

His batting eye was practically perfect; it is said that his eyesight was so good he could figure out which way a pitch was spinning before he began his swing. He was a strict pull hitter (that is, as a left-handed hitter, he hit most of his balls to right field; a righty pull hitter usually hits to left field), but would adjust his swing when absolutely necessary—such as in 1946, when he hit a ball down the third-base line and wound up with an inside-the-park home run to clinch the American League pennant. It was the only pennant the Red Sox won in his 17 full seasons with the team.

Williams' career statistics—including 521 home runs and 1,839 RBI—are doubly impressive when you consider that he spent three years in the military. From 1943–45 he was a pilot and a flight instructor in the Navy. Later, during the Korean War, he rejoined, this time with the Marines, and became a jet fighter pilot. His uncanny eyesight made him a fine airman as well as a tremendous batsman. He was good young and old, with 145 RBI for the Red Sox at the age of 21, and a .316 average at the age of 42. Appropriately, he hit a home run in his final at-bat on September 28, 1960.

G.I. Joe (and Airman Ted)

The war presented a problem for millions of Americans, including athletes. Were they needed at home, where they had families and job commitments, or should they fight for the Allies in Europe or the Pacific? Baseball's biggest stars, Joe DiMaggio and Ted Williams, both accepted deferments that kept them out of the military. (Deferments are rules set up to let people who have other important roles in society avoid the danger of military service.) The 25-year-old Williams was the sole supporter of his divorced mother, while 28-year-old DiMaggio had a wife and an infant.

But they were criticized in the newspapers and occasionally reprimanded by fans, and the pressure finally got to be too much. Soon after the end of the 1942 season, DiMaggio joined the Army as a sergeant and Williams entered Navy flight school. Each lost three prime seasons, though neither saw actual combat time during the war.

Frozen Gloves

Although most sports continued to be played as America entered the war, the National Boxing Association concluded that boxing was inappropriate. So the association froze all titles on October 16 and encouraged its competitors to join the military effort, even if it was only to promote physical education, sell war bonds, or put on boxing exhibitions to lift the morale of the troops.

Joe Louis, the renowned heavyweight champion, joined the Army on January 10.

While he never came close to any whizzing bullets, he proved to be a tireless and important participant. Over his four-year tour of duty, Louis traveled more than 70,000 miles and fought 96 exhibition matches. In 1944 he starred in *The Negro Soldier*, a film directed by Frank Capra that was designed to encourage African Americans to enlist in the military.

More important than the diversion he offered were the cultural changes Louis helped effect. Assigned to a base at Fort Riley, Kansas, in 1942, he met a young college football star and soldier named Jackie Robinson, who later joined Louis

G.I. Joe *Boxer Joe Louis enlisted in the Army. He spent his service fighting not at the front, but in the ring.*

1942

as one of the decade's towering sports figures. Robinson complained that he and 18 other black soldiers were being improperly denied entrance into the officer-candidate program.

Louis took up the issue with Truman Gibson, special advisor on Negro affairs to the secretary of war, and with Brigadier General Donald A. Robinson, commanding officer of the Cavalry Training Center at Fort Riley. Louis even threatened to pull out of his scheduled exhibitions, and Robinson and his comrades were admitted to officer-candidate schools within a week. All became officers.

On another occasion, a British theater denied Louis admission, explaining that the American commanding officer gave an order prohibiting his white and black soldiers from attending movies together. Louis complained, and a superior officer revoked the order. He also fired the commanding officer. "If whites and blacks were all fighting the same war," Louis asked, "why couldn't their morale be lifted at the same theater?"

Louis was honorably discharged from the Army in 1945, taking with him a Legion of Merit award for his service.

Redskins' Revenge

The Chicago Bears' 73–0 romp in the 1940 NFL Championship Game propelled the team to a new level of confidence. The Bears won the title again in 1941, and looked even stronger in 1942 as they went 11–0 and outscored their op-

Our Man in St. Louis

Watching young Stan Musial stride to the plate for another appearance at Ebbets Field, the Brooklyn Dodgers fans could only sigh, "Here comes that man again." On the road or at home in St. Louis, he became "Stan the Man," one of baseball's most beloved players.

Musial's career with the Cardinals lasted 22 seasons. Using an unconventional, corkscrewed batting stance, he was a rare combination of power and contact, a man who blasted 475 career home runs yet hit .310 or better in each of his first 16 full seasons.

Musial turned down a basketball scholarship to the University of Pittsburgh in 1938, opting to sign with the Cardinals as a left-handed pitcher. A shoulder injury ended that dream, but he got his chance as a hitter when he was called up from a minor-league team late in 1941. By 1943 he was voted Most Valuable Player of the National League.

Stan the Man retired with more than two dozen National League records. He was the first player to log 1,000 games at each of two positions—outfield and first base. He played in 24 All-Star Games (there were two per season from 1959 to 1962), and his statue now stands in front of Busch Stadium in St. Louis.

As longtime broadcaster Harry Carey said, "He was the greatest star—the character, the soul, the accessibility. Nobody combined that with as much baseball greatness as Musial."

Other Milestones of 1942

✔ The NHL discontinued regular-season overtime games because of wartime blackout restrictions.

✔ Stanford University defeated Dartmouth College 53–38 to win the NCAA basketball championship in March.

✔ The Indianapolis 500 was canceled due to the war and gasoline rationing.

✔ Golfer Byron Nelson won his second Master's tournament in April, edging Ben Hogan.

✔ Swimmer Gloria Callen was the Associated Press female athlete of the year.

Frank Sinkwich

✔ Frank Sinkwich, the University of Georgia's electrifying halfback, won the Heisman Trophy, given to college football's best player. Soon after, he enlisted in the Marines.

---

ponents 376–84. The team known as the "Monsters of the Midway" seemed to be invincible in every way.

The Washington Redskins also had an impressive season in 1942, finishing 10–1. But bettors made them 22-point underdogs in the 1942 Championship Game on December 13. Chicago, after all, had won 24 consecutive games, if you include postseason and preseason. Plus, nobody believed Washington could mentally recover from the historic beating it had taken two seasons earlier.

Sure enough, the Bears went up 6–0 in the second quarter, scoring when 230-pound tackle Lee Artoe picked up a fumble and ran 50 yards for a touchdown. But the Redskins stiffened. They answered the Bears with a 38-yard touchdown pass from Sammy Baugh to Wilbur Moore, then added a short plunge over the goal line by Andy Farkas in the third quarter. Washington's underrated defense didn't allow another point. The final was 14–6.

Baugh completed five of 13 passes for 66 yards, nowhere near his usual production. But the versatile star made one of the game's biggest defensive plays, intercepting a pass in the end zone.

Another Chicago drive ended on downs after officials called back a touchdown because of a penalty. "I guess this kinda makes up for that thing in 1940," Baugh said afterward.

1943

Sports and the War

By 1943, World War II had affected every part of American life. Sports was no exception. Major League Baseball had to change the balls themselves, for instance. The bits of rubber normally used were needed for use by the military, so baseball used blatta, another gummy substance. Whether because of the modified ball or because so many of the game's best hitters were in military uniform, offense sagged. In 1944, the New York Yankees' Nick Etten led the American League with a mere 22 home runs.

College football may have been hit hardest. By 1943, more than 300 colleges had abandoned the sport, including such powerhouses as the University of Alabama, Stanford University, Fordham University, and Georgetown University.

The 1943 Army–Navy game, meanwhile, was played at the West Point (New York) Army Academy, rather than its usual big-city venue. The academy limited tickets to on-duty Army personnel and civilians living within 10 miles of the stadium. Several U.S. Congressmen protested, but under-secretary of war Robert P. Patterson remained firm, saying it was necessary "because of transportation and fuel shortages."

In the NFL, retired players returned to fill spots created by current players joining the military. Bronko Nagurski hadn't played in five seasons. But the Chicago Bears coaxed the legendary fullback out of retirement at the age of 34, and he helped them to their third championship in four years.

Even golf, that supposed refuge of the upper class, felt the pinch. By 1943, Sam

Crowned in Absentia

In 1943, no college football player could escape the shadow of "Accurate" Angelo Bertelli, dynamic quarterback of the top-ranked Fighting Irish of the University of Notre Dame. But Bertelli got his draft notice just after midseason and spent the rest of the schedule in Marine boot camp at Parris Island Marine Base in South Carolina.

Amazingly, Bertelli won the Heisman Trophy, anyway. The vote wasn't even close. He was unable to attend the award ceremony on December 3, though. He was busy cleaning his rifle and doing push-ups in the dirt.

You Go, Girls *Women got their chance on the diamond during World War II with their own pro baseball league.*

Snead, Jimmy Demaret, Lloyd Mangrum, and other top golfers were in the armed forces. Mangrum, in fact, was wounded twice during the Battle of the Bulge.

Diamonds Are a Girl's Best Friend

Fans looking for pro baseball were left with teams that were a far cry from their pre-war rosters. To fill baseball fans' need for the game—and with an eye toward making some money—Philip K. Wrigley, owner of the Chicago Cubs, tried something new. He noted a boom in women's softball and so he started the All-American Girls Softball League, composed of the Kenosha (Wisconsin) Comets, the Racine (Wisconsin) Belles, the Rockford (Illinois) Peaches, and the South Bend (Indiana) Blue Sox.

At first, the league used a 12-inch ball and pitched it underhand. But it soon changed into true baseball, and in 1945 the league changed the word Softball in its name to Baseball. The only difference

1943

from the men's game—besides the pastel skirts—was a smaller diamond, with 72 feet between bases instead of 90. These short base paths helped Sophie Kurys steal 201 bases in 203 attempts in 1943.

This was an era when women flooded into jobs traditionally occupied by their husbands and brothers, including heavy manufacturing. Some men worried about a loss of femininity, and Wrigley insisted that his players adhere to a strictly lady-like image. This theme was continued by advertising executive Arthur Meyerhoff, who purchased Wrigley's share in 1944.

Wrigley and Meyerhoff instructed scouts to weigh both physical appearance and ability when evaluating prospects. In spring training of 1943 and 1944, the league sent its athletes to an evening charm school conducted by Helena Rubinstein's well-known Chicago beauty salon. They were coached on subjects such as posture, fashion, applying make-up, and table manners.

A dress code distributed in 1951 read, "Masculine hair styling, shoes, coats, shirts, socks, T-shirts are barred at all times." Getting ejected from a game cost a player a $10 fine ($10 was a lot for women making $50 to $85 per week); appearing "unkempt" in public drew an even stiffer penalty. Each team had a chaperone to ensure proper behavior.

"When I first started, I thought, 'Gosh, how the heck are we going to play ball in those things?'" Racine's Anna May Hutchison said of the skirts. "But once you got used to them they were just your uniform and that was it."

In general, the AAGBL was a huge hit. The league successfully expanded to small industrial centers such as Kalamazoo and Battle Creek, Michigan; Fort Wayne, Indiana; and Peoria, Illinois. (It did not fare as well in larger cities such as Chicago and Milwaukee.) Attendance grew annually until it peaked in 1948, when the 10-team league drew almost a million fans. It even spawned a rival, the National Girls Baseball League.

Popularity declined after that, however, as the novelty wore off and fans either returned to men's baseball or stayed home to watch the new medium of television. The AAGBL folded after the 1954 season. Curiously, the league that opened so many doors for female athletes was extremely slow to hire African Americans.

Sugar and the Bull

Everyone associated with boxing respected the skills of Sugar Ray Robinson, but Jake LaMotta, who spent time in reform school before entering the ring and becoming the "Bronx Bull," never feared him. The two boxers tangled six times over their careers, and each fight seemed to be bloodier and more intense than the last. "I fought Sugar so often, I almost got diabetes," LaMotta joked.

Robinson, who usually fought as a welterweight, beat LaMotta, a middleweight, in 1942. He defeated plenty of other foes, too. He was, in fact, 40–0 (with 29 knockouts) when he met LaMotta again on February 5, 1943. This time the Bronx Bull handed Robinson his first professional loss, taking a 10-round decision. Barely three weeks later, February 26, Robinson won a decision over LaMotta in another 10-rounder.

The two met twice again in 1945. And on February 14, 1951, before 15,000 fans in Chicago, welterweight champion Robinson beat middleweight champion LaMotta in a 13th-round technical knockout, claiming his second championship belt. By the end of the fight, now called the "Valentine's Day Massacre," the Bronx Bull was hardly able to raise his hands in defense.

"Jake was the toughest guy I ever fought," Robinson said. "I hit him with everything, and he'd just act like you're crazy. I never did knock him off his feet." Robinson did, however, serve as LaMotta's best man when his rival got married late in life.

Ride 'em, Cowboys!

Basketball, especially on the high school and collegiate levels, always has been associated with the Midwest. Powerful teams had emerged on both coasts in the 1930s. But it wasn't until 1943 that the Rocky Mountain zone made its mark. The team that did it was the Cowboys of the University of Wyoming.

The Cowboys were coached by Ev Shelton, who took over the program in 1939. Shelton won 328 games with the Cowboys, and after his death was elected to the National Basketball Hall of Fame.

The 1943 squad was Shelton's crowning glory. The team was led by Kenny

Sugar Was One Sweet Boxer

Sugar Ray Robinson brought life to boxing's oldest cliché of being "pound for pound" the greatest fighter ever. He was born Walker Smith, Jr., on May 3, 1921, in the same impoverished Detroit neighborhood that produced Joe Louis. He became "Ray Robinson" when he borrowed a friend's union card for an amateur boxing tournament. The "Sugar" came from New York City gym owner George Gainford, who tried to explain how sweet the moves of his young fighter were.

(109 by knockout) and claiming six world championships. In 202 career fights, he failed to go the distance only once.

"Robinson could deliver a knockout blow going backward," Bert Sugar wrote in The Ring. "His footwork was superior to any that had been seen up to that time."

Robinson was a flamboyant character who drove a pink Cadillac, owned a Harlem, New York, nightclub, and traveled around Europe with a

Robinson had a very long career, unusual for an athlete in such a physically demanding sport. He fought professionally for 25 years, winning 175 fights large entourage that included a valet, a barber, and a mascot who was a dwarf. He made a lot of money and spent every penny of it.

1943

Sailors, still the only player in Wyoming basketball history to earn All-America honors three times. A native of Hillsdale, Wyoming, Sailors is credited (by some, anyway) with inventing the jump shot; certainly his success helped popularize the shot (before then, players normally shot while standing on the floor). Sailors was the college basketball player of the year in 1943.

The Cowboys breezed through a 31–2 season, even though they played just nine home games. The only games they lost were to Duquesne, early in the schedule, and the Denver Legion team. They beat Regis 101–45, an unlikely score in that slow-paced era. The NCAA tournament in March proved to be a tough ride, though. Wyoming scraped by in its first two games, beating Oklahoma 53–50 and Texas 58–54. The championship game was more one-sided. The Cowboys beat Georgetown 46–34, and Sailors was named the tournament MVP.

Two days later, Wyoming faced off with St. John's University, the NIT champion, in a benefit game for the Red Cross. This one went into overtime, but Wyoming again came out on top, 52–47 in hostile Madison Square Garden in New York.

Sailors then left for two years of military service, but returned to gain further All-America recognition in 1946.

Hostilities at Home

World War II had a terrible effect on Europe, as millions lost their lives and hundreds of cities and towns were destroyed or damaged. The changes in America were not as violent, but they were enormous. More than 1.6 million people moved from the South to find work and housing in northern cities that were home to war-materials factories. Many of these uprooted families were African-American, and the demographic shift was not always a smooth one.

In Detroit, called the "arsenal of democracy" at the time because of its munitions plants, interracial tension heated to the boiling point. A riot erupted in June, and Briggs Stadium was right in the middle of the violence. On June 23, the Detroit Tigers and Cleveland Indians played a baseball doubleheader with 350 armed troops stationed in the stands.

The riots finally ended with 34 people dead, 700 injured, and 1,200 in jail. Clearly, Nazi Germany was not the only country struggling with issues of race and identity.

The Other Arms Race

As the season wore on, more and more players left their Major League Baseball teams to join various branches of the military. Still, some teams managed to keep enough players to remain at the top of the league. The New York Yankees lost most of their top hitters to the services, but their outstanding pitching staff stayed home. Spud Chandler was particularly successful, going 20–4 with a league-best ERA of 1.64 in 1943. Starting pitchers Ernie Bonham and Hank Borowy also stayed with the Yankees.

Likewise, the St. Louis Cardinals had a fairly full complement of arms. In fact, the top three pitchers in the National League in ERA were all Cardinals: Howie Pollet, Max Lanier, and Mort Cooper. Cooper went 21–8, maintaining his position as the league's most feared thrower. St. Louis also had Stan Musial, who hit .357.

Another Battle   *Teams like Iowa Preflight (in the dark uniforms) were cheered on by stands filled with Navy men.*

The Yankees won the American League pennant by 13 1/2 games, the Cardinals took the National League flag by 18 games, and the two teams faced off in October in a World Series rematch.

This time, New York turned the tables. A year earlier, St. Louis committed 10 errors but still managed to win four of five games. The Cardinals made 10 errors in five games again, and this year it cost them. Compounding the defensive lapses was a lack of timely hitting; St. Louis left 37 runners on base in five games in the Fall Classic.

Chandler pitched two complete games and surrendered only one earned run. The Yankees' Marius Russo, who went 5–10 during the season, started game four, pitched a complete game, and scored the winning run when he doubled and came home on a sacrifice fly by shortstop Frankie Crosetti.

In this pitcher-dominated era, the two teams combined to hit a mere .222 in the Series.

Go Iowa Preflight!

To play or not to play? That was the question faced by America's college coaches and military leaders. Some felt that sports helped prepare soldiers for physical work as well as teamwork. Others thought that sports took attention away from vital work for the war. One supporter of college sports was Commander Tom Hamilton, head of the U.S. Navy and Marine Corps. Hamilton advocated football, in particular, as a form of combat preparation. So colleges with

1943

Naval training programs were allowed to suit up sailors in football uniforms.

What's more, many Navy and Marine bases fielded their own teams. And they were among the best in the nation. In 1943, the Associated Press Top 20 College Football Teams included Iowa Preflight, Great Lakes Naval Station, Del Monte Preflight, March Field, and Bainbridge Navy Training School. Randolph Field tied a strong University of Texas team in the Cotton Bowl in January.

The next year, four of those teams made the Top 20 again (all but Del Monte), along with Randolph Field, Norman Preflight, El Toro Marines, Fort Pierce, St. Mary's Preflight, and Second Air Force. The 1944 bowl lineup included something called the Treasury Bowl, with Randolph Field defeating Second Air Force 13–6.

Triple Threat

By 1943, Sammy Baugh clearly was the best overall player in the NFL. While leading the Washington Redskins, the agile passer from Texas was, without question, the league's first great quarterback. His skills and leadership made Washington a perennial contender. In 1943, however, Baugh outdid even his own amazing accomplishments. He set a standard for all-around football skill that has never been matched.

First he set a league record with six touchdown passes against the Brooklyn Dodgers (an NFL team from 1930 to 1944 that played under the same name as the local baseball team). Two weeks later he set another record by intercepting four passes from his safety position.

When the season was over, Baugh wound up leading the league in passing (a completion rate of 56 percent), interceptions (11), and punting (45.9-yard average). It was a rare football Triple Crown. Longtime *Sports Illustrated* writer Peter King called it "the best season a pro football player ever had." No player since has ever led the league in even two of those categories in a career, let alone a season.

Baugh took Washington to the 1943 NFL Championship Game. But he got kicked in the head while making a tackle in the first half, and missed much of the game. The Chicago Bears won 41–21 on December 26.

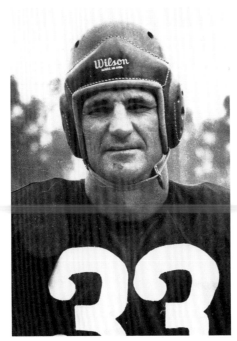

Mr. Everything *Sammy Baugh of the Redskins was the NFL's best passer, punter, and defensive back in 1943.*

Other Milestones of 1943

✔ Count Fleet, ridden by jockey Johnny Longden, became the sixth horse ever to win the Triple Crown, capturing the Kentucky Derby, Preakness Stakes, and Belmont Stakes—which he won by 25 lengths.

✔ Relief pitcher Ace Adams set a 20th-century record by pitching in 70 baseball games for the New York Giants. He pitched a complete game in

Johnny Longden on Count Fleet

only one of them. (The record is now held by relief pitcher Mike Marshall of the Los Angeles Dodgers, who pitched in 106 games in 1974.)

✔ In a cold, steady rain, the New York Giants and Detroit Lions battled through the NFL's last scoreless tie on November 7. Neither team's offense drove inside the opponent's 15-yard line.

Steagles and Carpets

How did the NFL cope with the loss of players to the military? Like other leagues, it had smaller rosters for every team. However, two teams lost so many players, they almost couldn't play. What they did instead was cooperate in difficult times in a way that would probably shock modern sports team owners.

Instead of the Philadelphia Eagles and Pittsburgh Steelers cancelling their 1943 seasons, they merged for one year. The "new" team was officially known as the Phil–Pitt Eagles–Steelers. Sports fans quickly dubbed them the Steagles.

Philadelphia's Earle Neale and Pittsburgh's Walt Kiesling shared the head-coaching duties. Neale directed the offense, Kiesling the defense, and they barely kept their hands off one another's throats. Neale cursed a mistake-prone Steelers' player at one practice, and Kiesling pulled all the Steelers off the field.

Not surprisingly, the two coaches never became friends.

The players were required to work at least 40 hours a week in factories making armaments. They trained at the University of Pennsylvania six evenings a week. "You worked all day, and you practiced all night, and by the end of the day you were tired as hell," Hinkle said.

The Steagles were surprisingly good in 1943. They went 5–4–1. Hinkle led a strong ground attack with 571 yards rushing.

The merger officially ended on the final day of the season. The Eagles flew solo in 1944 and narrowly missed the Eastern Division title with a record of 7–1–2. The Steelers, however, still needed help. This time they merged with the Chicago Cardinals, forming a conglomerate that stumbled to an 0–10 record, getting outscored 328–108 along the way. The name of this team was Card–Pitt. To fans, they would always be the Carpets.

1944

A Little Less Than Usual

By this year, the events of World War II were drawing to a close. Among the most important military moments were the bombing of Tokyo in April and Allied forces' landing on the French beach of Normandy on June 6. Events in the world of sports continued to be trivial in comparison. However, the games did go on, even if the players were not quite all Major League quality.

Only 40 percent of the players who had started on Opening Day of 1941 were around to do the same in 1944. All nine of the New York Yankees' 1941 starters had gone to war. To fill in, many teams welcomed back aging stars. Once-speedy outfielder Johnny Martin returned to the St. Louis Cardinals for 40 games at the age of 40. He hit .279 after a three-year absence. Jimmie Foxx (1907–1967), one of the all-time great hitters, rejoined the Chicago Cubs. The next year he even pitched for the Philadelphia Phillies. One measure of the talent drain during the war: Foxx posted a very low ERA of 1.59 in 22 2/3 innings.

It wasn't just veterans. The Cincinnati Reds set a record that still stands by putting a 15-year-old pitcher on the mound. Joe Nuxhall's first appearance was about what you would expect from a kid too young to drive—five runs and five walks surrendered in two-thirds of an inning. Nuxhall didn't appear in another major league game for eight years, but then fashioned a solid pro career, mostly with the Reds.

One owner was so distraught about the sad state of Major League play that he suggested they just stop playing. Alva Bradley, owner of the Cleveland Indians, agreed with Spink. He urged his fellow team owners to suspend operations in 1944, and for the remainder of the war, describing the baseball of the era as "a low form of comedy." The other owners sternly shot down the idea.

Beware the Blitz

The University of Utah basketball team had no shortage of hurdles to overcome during the 1943–44 season. The players were young (most of them under 19 years old) and not particularly tall (averaging six feet). They also had no conference (it had dissolved during the war) and no gymnasium (the Army took it over). The Utes practiced in local church gyms.

A Separate Game   *Forced into internment camps, Japanese Americans still played baseball (page 44).*

They overcame all of it with flair, and pretty soon people were calling them the Blitz Kids. After charging through a regular-season schedule that included many armed-forces teams, Utah declined an NCAA tournament bid and joined a strong field in the National Invitation Tournament (NIT). There they fell to University of Kentucky, 46–38 on March 26.

The Utes weren't finished in 1944, though. When the University of Arkansas bowed out of the NCAA tournament in March, organizers again invited Utah.

This time the school accepted, and it rolled to the title game, where it outlasted Dartmouth College 42–40.

But even that was not the end of the season. A Red Cross benefit game in April paired the champions of each tournament. So Utah got a shot at St. John's University, which had won the NIT. The Utes won 43–36, led by freshman All-American Arnie Ferrin's 17 points.

It was a strange path to the top of the college basketball world, but Utah was happy to be there.

Helping at Home

The sports world came to the aid of the war effort in a number of interesting ways. Of course, the major form of aid came from the athletes themselves, many of whom served with distinction. Other ways sports helped out included:

- Players visited factories to cheer workers and promote the sale of war bonds.

- Soldiers and other military members were welcome free at all ballparks. More than 4.5 million took advantage of the offer.

- Teams held "salvage days," at which fans could get into games free if they brought scrap metal, kitchen fat, or scrap paper to donate.

- More than 75 percent of all sports equipment was provided to military teams.

- At Major League Baseball stadiums, foul balls were often retrieved and sent to military bases to be used by soldiers. The proceeds from the 1942 All-Star Game also helped provide bats, balls, and other equipment for fighting men and women.

Baseball in the Camps

In 1944, baseball was the game that best defined and united Americans. It was an ironic and poignant twist, then, that baseball flourished in a most unlikely place—the internment camps built for Japanese Americans.

Fueled by shrill newspaper commentaries, racism, and a general feeling of paranoia, President Roosevelt signed Executive Order 9066 in February 1942, which mandated the mass eviction and incarceration of all people of Japanese descent living on the West Coast. By October of that year, most of these American citizens had been assigned to 10 internment camps—infamous and desolate places such as Manzanar and Tule Lake in California, and Gila River in Arizona.

Baseball was extremely popular in Japan, and had long been important in the Japanese-American community, so the detainees immediately set about constructing fields and ordering equipment from mail-order catalogs.

"Right near our block was an open space, so we started digging out the sagebrush from the desert floor," recalled Howard Zenimura, whose father, Kenichi, designed the baseball diamond at Gila River. "Pretty soon people came by to ask us what we were doing. We told them we were building a ballpark, and then everybody was out there with their shovels clearing that space."

Most of the diamonds were actually built outside the barbed wire of the camps. (With hundreds of miles of desert in every direction, it did not seem to matter.) Some camp teams were allowed to travel for exhibition games, while others welcomed teams from outside the camps. The games were highlights of an otherwise dreary existence.

There were 32 teams, split among three divisions, at Gila River alone. The Tule Lake Baseball Convention, which began May 2, 1944, attracted more than 9,000 fans.

Of course, devotion to baseball was not the only example of Japanese-American loyalty. The 100th Infantry Battalion, made up of second-generation Nisei from Hawaii, was among the most decorated U.S. Army units of its size.

Meet Me in St. Louis

If the wartime manpower shortage lowered the level of Major League Baseball play, at least it leveled the playing field. And that was good news for the St. Louis Browns, the American League's most downtrodden team.

Entering the 1944 season, the Browns had enjoyed exactly one winning year in their last 14. During the 1930s they had lost 90 or more games in eight of 10 years. In 1944 the St. Louis players averaged nearly 32 years of age. The Browns had no stars. Yet by season's end they had edged the Detroit Tigers by a game and won the A.L. pennant.

With the Cardinals claiming their third straight National League pennant, the World Series became an all-St. Louis affair. Opposing managers Billy Southworth (Cardinals) and Luke Sewell (Browns), because of the wartime housing shortage, actually shared an apartment. All six games were played in October at Sportsman's Park.

The Browns played tough and took a lead of two games to one. After that, Harry "The Cat" Breechen and the splendid Mort Cooper pitched complete games for the Cardinals to win games four and five, and reliever Ted Wilks retired the last 11 Browns in the sixth game. Where the Cardinals' defense had abandoned them against the Yankees in 1942 and 1943, this time they made only one error, while it was the American Leaguers who committed 10.

The Browns returned to their losing ways by 1946, and remained in or near the basement until moving to Baltimore and becoming the Orioles in 1954.

Kids Behaving Badly

College basketball was gaining popularity in the mid-1940s. But the game was rocked on October 2 when "Phog" Allen (1885–1974) of the University of Kansas, one of the nation's most respected coaches, charged that gamblers were inducing college players to throw games (to lose intentionally) or shave points (win, but score fewer points—a benefit to gamblers). Allen warned of "a scandal that will stink to high heaven." But college presidents took no action.

Two-Armed Tigers

The Detroit Tigers' Paul "Dizzy" Trout and Hal Newhouser were an unstoppable one-two pitching combination in 1944. Newhouser, known as "Prince Hal,", had a 29–9 record with an ERA of 2.22. Trout's numbers were 27–14 and 2.12. Together they combined for a staggering 664 innings and 58 complete games.

Alas, Trout and Newhouser got little help from the rest of the team's pitching staff. No other Tigers' pitcher even had a winning record in 1944, and the team finished one game out of first place.

1944

The Kansas coach was right. In January 1945, five Brooklyn College players admitted to accepting bribes. In time, four other New York-area colleges were hit by similar accusations. And it wasn't just a Big Apple problem. Bradley University (in Peoria, Illinois) and University of Toledo (in Ohio) eventually got sucked into the scandal, followed by the mighty University of Kentucky in 1951.

By the time the sport was cleaned up, eight colleges and about 40 players were implicated.

Invincible Army

At a time when most colleges were struggling just to find players for their teams, the Army had an advantage. If an active serviceman had previous college playing experience, the U.S. Military Academy could offer him three more years of athletic eligibility and keep him out of the draft until graduation. In exchange, the athletes were required to cram their four-year officers' training into three years. Few could resist the deal.

These uneven standards gave Army a powerful team in an era of shaky squads, and the result was fearsome to behold.

The Black Knights of Army, coached by Colonel Earl "Red" Blaik (1897–1989), simply crushed the opposition in 1944. They won with scores such as 83–0, 76–0, and 62–7. Even mighty Notre Dame stood no chance. Army beat the defending national champion 59–0 to hand the Fighting Irish its worst loss ever.

The Black Knights' biggest test came against archrival Navy, which entered the game ranked second after Army. The game was close until the fourth quarter, when fullback Felix "Doc" Blanchard (1924–2009) powered one touchdown drive and halfback Glenn Davis (1924–2005) capped another with a 50-yard sprint. Army prevailed 23–7.

Army was so loaded with talent in 1944 that Blanchard and Davis—known as

Water Star *Named the top athlete in America for 1944, the multitalented swimmer Ann Curtis would go on to win 31 national championships at a variety of distances.*

Other Milestones of 1944

✔ The NCAA/AAU (Amateur Athletic Union) Joint Basketball Rules Committee outlawed goaltending—interfering with a shot after the ball has begun the downward part of its arc toward the basket—unless the shot is clearly short of the basket.

✔ Robert Hamilton, a relative unknown, beat golf legend Byron Nelson by a shot in the PGA Championship tournament in August.

Curly Lambeau

✔ On June 10, a rare triple tie ended a horse race at the Aqueduct race track in Long Island, New York. Bossuet, Brownie, and Wait a Bit crossed the finish line simultaneously in the Carter Handicap.

✔ The NFL legalized coaching from the bench. Before the change, coaches (such as Curly Lambeau of Green Bay, pictured at left) could not yell instructions to their players on the field.

"Mr. Inside and Mr. Outside"—were not in the regular starting lineup. As freshmen, they left that honor to the upperclassmen. Still, they got enough carries to rush for 1,002 yards between them, and Davis set an NCAA record with 20 touchdowns in a single season.

Curts Swims to the Top

The nuns of Ursuline Convent School in Santa Rosa, California, taught Ann Curtis how to swim. Curtis was born in 1926, and by the age of 11 she won a freestyle race for girls under 16. Her mother held her out of major adult competition until 1943. The next year, her career took off.

Curtis won the Amateur Athletic Union (AAU) national outdoor swimming championships in the 100 meters, the 400 meters, the 800 meters, and the one mile.

Indoors she claimed the 220-yard and 440-yard races.

Curtis was a national sensation at the age of 18, and the AAU acknowledged it by awarding her the 1944 Sullivan Award (named for James E. Sullivan, who founded the AAU in 1888) as the top overall athlete. She was the first woman to win the award since its inception in 1930, and she'd be the only one to claim the honor until diver Patricia McCormick in 1956. She also was named female athlete of the year by Associated Press in 1944.

The only thing that took away from Curtis' amazing year was the cancellation of the 1944 Summer Olympics in London. She would have been favored to win several gold medals. Curtis got her chance in London in 1948, and swam well enough to win individual gold and silver medals and also a relay gold.

1945

War and Peace

By 1945, the tide of World War II had turned in favor of the Allied forces. But the fighting remained heavy early in the year, and the toll back home was as severe as ever.

The 1945 All-Star Game was canceled at the government's request. Meanwhile, the Brooklyn Dodgers signed Floyd "Babe" Herman, a one-time star who hadn't played in eight seasons (he was now 42). Hod Lisenbee pitched for the Cincinnati Reds in 1945, at the age of 46. The Detroit Tigers were jokingly called the Nine Old Men. They averaged nearly 35 years in age. Experience paid off, however, when they won the 1945 World Series over the Chicago Cubs.

But none of the stories epitomized the lean mid-40s better than that of Pete Gray. The outfielder appeared in 77 games for the St. Louis Browns, hitting .218 and striking out only 11 times in 234 at-bats. Not bad for a man with one arm.

Gray had lost his arm in a farm accident. He played with a tiny glove. He would catch the ball, toss it up, drop the glove, grab the ball, and then throw it. He was an inspiration to many.

Playing Over There

For nearly four years, America's fighting forces obtained hope and relief from the stress of battle through spectator sports. As the war wound down, some of those soldiers got their own opportunities to play ball.

Soon after the liberation of Rome on June 4, 1944, for example, officials organized a Spaghetti Bowl football game. Less than three weeks after Japan signed articles of surrender aboard the *USS Missouri* on September 2, officially ending World War II, *The New York Times* announced that the winner of the Mediterranean Theater baseball championship would meet the winner of the European Theater in a best-of-five series. And in October the 508th Parachute Regiment met a U.S. Air Force team in a football game held in Frankfurt on the Main, Germany. Some 20,000 soldiers were on hand to watch the action.

Many American soldiers remained in Europe even after the war was over, leading to further sporting events in 1946. The Spaghetti Bowl returned, this time in Florence, where it attracted 25,000 spectators. There was also a GI World Series for

TRANS-LUX PRESENTS A SPECIAL V-J DAY PROGRAM

Peace *This couple celebrates the end of hostilities in the East: Victory in Japan (V-J) Day.*

the championship of occupied Germany, with the 60th Infantry Regiment of the 9th Division winning four of six games against the 508th Parachute Regiment. Right-hander Carl Scheib won two games in the GI World Series, then went on to win 45 games with the Philadelphia Athletics in the late 1940s and early 1950s.

The ultimate expression of sports-as-triumph came in 1945, though. That was when American soldiers who had recently liberated Berlin at the end of the long war etched a baseball diamond into the field of Nuremberg Stadium, where huge Nazi rallies had so recently honored Adolf Hitler.

1945

Bob the Big Boy

In an era when many basketball centers stood 6-foot-5 or 6-foot-6, 7-footer Bob Kurland was a giant among men. The NCAA had outlawed his goal-tending defense in 1944 (see page 47), but Kurland was smooth enough to adjust.

In 1945, Oklahoma A&M coach Hank Iba (1904–1993) assembled enough talent around his big man to make a serious NCAA tournament run. (Iba coached at the school, later known as Oklahoma State University, for 35 years.) The A&M Aggies won the championship by beating New York University 49–45 in March. Kurland was named most valuable player of the tournament. More important to the future of the sport, he threw down the first authenticated slam dunk. He called it his "duffer shot."

Oklahoma A&M was even better the following year, when five war veterans came home to join the five returning starters. Kurland led the team in scoring, had 72 points in three tournament games, and sparked a 43–40 victory over University of North Carolina in the NCAA final in March. The Aggies were the first college basketball team ever to win consecutive NCAA championships.

One a Game

Maurice Richard's blazing goal scoring for the Montreal Canadiens in the 1944 NHL postseason had made him a folk hero in Quebec. Kids now wore his number-9 jersey and greased their hair so they would look just like the Rocket.

In 1945, Richard stretched his remarkable performance over an entire regular season. He exhausted defenders and skillfully handled the passes of his Canadiens teammates Toe Blake and Elmer Lach, lighting up scoreboards from Chicago to Boston. Richard scored his record-breaking 44th goal in his 40th game of the season.

Going into the last game of the season, he had 49 goals. The March 18 contest

He Shoots . . . He Scores! *Maurice Richard (at right, shown here with his brother Henri) rewrote the hockey record books with his amazing goal-a-game pace in the 1944–45 season.*

The Mahatma

Branch Rickey had a bigger effect on baseball than just about any other person in the 20th century. He started as a player, but made his real mark as a developer of players, an organizer of teams, and as a baseball innovator.

As the general manager of the St. Louis Cardinals, he created the farm system of minor-league teams. On those clubs, often owned or at least supported by Major League teams, developing players could hone their skills before joining the big club. Rickey also dreamed up batting cages, sliding pits, and Ladies'

Day (a special promotion to get women to come to the ballpark). In his most groundbreaking move, while running the Brooklyn Dodgers, he set about plotting the demise of the color barrier that had kept African Americans out of Major League Baseball for nearly half a century. The man called "the Mahatma" for his wisdom and serious manner left a vast imprint on the game.

"In breaking down the color barrier in baseball, he did more for the Negroes than any white man since Abraham Lincoln," Jackie Robinson wrote.

---

was broadcast by radio across Canada and followed by dispatch among Canadian soldiers abroad. Richard scored one goal against the Boston Bruins and finished with 50 goals in 50 games—something no man had done since the modern NHL was established in 1926.

It would, in fact, be the only one-goal-a-game pace over an NHL season until Wayne Gretzky (b.1961) repeated the feat in the 1981–82 season.

Inside, Outside, Winning Side

Anyone expecting the Army football team to fall back to earth was sorely disappointed. If anything, the Black Knights got better. Six of their opponents wound up in the final Associated Press Top 20, but the Knights treated them with no respect. The 1945 ledger included scores such as 61–0 over eighth-ranked University Pennsylvania, 54–0 over 19th-ranked Wake Forest University, and 48–0

over ninth-ranked University of Notre Dame. Over the course of two seasons, Army outscored its foes 916–81.

In 1945, halfback Glenn Davis and fullback Doc Blanchard fully took control of the backfield. Blanchard ("Mr. Inside") had played for the University of North Carolina (UNC) freshman squad in 1942. He tried to get into UNC's Navy V-12 program, but bad eyesight (a mud pie nailed him in the eye as a child) and a weight problem made him ineligible. The Army drafted him in 1943 and accepted him at West Point a year later. Blanchard ran for 718 yards, scored 19 touchdowns, leveled defenders with his crushing blocks, and won the Heisman Trophy in 1945. He also became the first football player to capture the Sullivan Award.

"Have just seen Superman in the flesh," one Notre Dame coach cabled back to South Bend, Indiana, after watching Army thrash Notre Dame in 1944. "He wears number 35 and goes by the name of Blanchard."

Saved from the Sand *Golfer Byron Nelson blasts out of a sand trap at the Riviera Country Club during the 1945 Los Angeles Open, one of an amazing 19 tournaments he won in his record-setting year.*

Full Nelson

Many of the nation's best golfers wound up fighting in World War II. Byron Nelson (b.1912) was not one of them. He was a hemophiliac, prone to excessive bleeding, and so was considered unfit for duty.

With the field diminished during the late stages of the conflict overseas, Nelson dominated the fairways as few golfers have. In 1944 he won seven tournaments, claimed more prize money than any other golfer, and averaged a crisp 69.67 strokes in 85 rounds of tournament play.

As great as that was, Nelson managed to get even better in 1945. The Texan won 19 of 31 tournaments, including 11 straight. His average for 120 tournament rounds was 68.33 strokes. He shot a blistering 62 in Seattle, Washington, tying an 18-hole tournament record, and broke the 72-hole mark with a 259.

Aging with Grace

Babe Didrikson was nothing new on the American sports scene by this time in her life. In 1932, she had dominated the Olympics, winning gold in the javelin and hurdles and silver in the high jump. This all-around athlete was also successful at basketball and softball. No other woman had ever been as good at so many sports as Babe.

As she got older, Didrikson turned her attention to golf. Not surprisingly, she soon established herself as the best female golfer in the world. In 1945 she won the first of three straight Associated Press Woman Athlete of the Year awards.

Davis ("Mr. Outside") was an all-around athlete from Southern California who was recruited by several Major League Baseball teams. He went to West Point as a freshman in 1943, after the academy promised to also take his twin brother. Davis was then expelled for academic problems, but was readmitted after completing a special four-month math class. His blazing speed helped him rack up 944 rushing yards and 18 touchdowns in 1945, although he would have to wait for 1946 to earn his Heisman.

Army was involved in one close contest in 1945. Giving in to popular demand, Coach Red Blaik let his A and B squads go at one another for 30 minutes of inspired competition at a practice in November. They scored three touchdowns each, but Blaik cut short the exhibition when All-America tackle DeWitt "Tex" Coulter tackled Davis at the sideline and drove him into a tackling dummy.

A Woman for All Seasons

Someone once asked Mildred "Babe" Didrikson (1915–1956) if there was anything she didn't play. "Yeah," she answered, "dolls."

It sometimes seemed that Didrikson could pick up any piece of sporting equipment and master it in a day. She was a champion runner, jumper, javelin thrower, and golfer in various stages of her career, always staying a step ahead of the pack.

At a time when "lady athletes" were expected to be sweet-natured, courteous, perhaps a little flirtatious, Didrikson was a true competitor. She flaunted and celebrated her athletic prowess and made little attempt to look pretty. And she took a beating for it, from a disapproving press that repeatedly questioned her lack of femininity.

In a supposedly supportive story about the athlete after her marriage to wrestler George Zaharias in 1935, *Life* magazine described a younger Didrikson as a girl whose "lips were too thin and her Adam's apple too big," and someone who "hated girls and only lived to beat them."

Didrikson didn't seem to care much. In fact, she loved the spotlight. A golfer who won 10 major tournaments, she was instrumental in founding the Ladies Professional Golf Association (LPGA) in 1949. The next year, the Associated Press voted her the Female American Athlete of the Half-Century. (Jim Thorpe was her male counterpart.) Didrikson contracted cancer and died in 1956, at the age of 45.

She was written and talked about in ways that would seem very inappropriate to today's readers. Female athletes had not yet achieved anywhere near the recognition and balance that they enjoy today. While still not equal to men, today's female athletes enjoy fame, some fortune, and fan support far above anything that Didrikson and her contemporaries received. Young women aspiring to a career in sports today can point to Babe and women like her as the pathfinders, the pioneers.

A crowd rings the green as Babe Didrikson (center) lines up a putt during a 1948 tournament.

1945

Didrikson, who won the prestigious Women's Western Open in both 1944 and 1945, also hinted that she might play golf in the all-male U.S. Open.

Reporters gobbled it up, and men were so spooked that the United States Golf Association (USGA) quickly assembled a meeting and explicitly barred women from the event. Officials then changed the name of the tournament to the U.S. Men's Open. Didrikson later told friends she was only joking.

Happy Hour

Until 1945, one man had been the face of baseball. Kenesaw Mountain Landis was named the sport's first commissioner in 1920 and had held office ever since. He was a towering figure who steered the Major Leagues through everything from the Black Sox betting scandal to World War II player shortages.

When Landis died on November 25, 1944, it left

the sport with a sizable power vacuum. The man the team owners selected to fill the hole was 46-year-old A.B. "Happy" Chandler (1898–1991), the former Kentucky governor and U.S. Senator. But the team owners felt he favored the players too much, and he was ousted after his seven-year term in 1951. Still, that was enough time for Chandler to oversee the revolution of African Americans playing in Major League Baseball.

Doink!

An hour before the first postwar NFL Championship Game, played December 16 game at Cleveland Municipal Stadium, the thermometer read three degrees below zero. By kickoff, that had climbed to a relatively balmy six degrees. Hoping to keep the field thawed, groundskeepers had scattered 9,000 bales of hay on the turf, creating four feet of insulation. They swept the hay to the sidelines just before pregame warm-ups. A few minutes into the game, however, the field was frozen solid.

The game pitted the hometown Rams against the Washington Redskins. "It was like trying to play on a paved surface," Washington quarterback Sammy Baugh said. "Like we were out in the street."

Baugh had bruised his ribs two weeks earlier. Now he and his counterpart, rookie quarterback Bob Waterfield (who was married to movie star Jane Russell), tried to deal with a vicious wind that blew off Lake Erie and prevented everyone from getting a solid grip on the ball. Players on the benches draped blankets over their legs to stave off numbness.

The game's pivotal play came early. The Redskins had just stopped Cleveland at the five-yard line when Baugh dropped back into his own end zone and fired a pass. Instead of arcing downfield, however, it clanged into one of the goal posts—which were set on the goal lines in those days. The officials ruled it a safety (when an offensive player is downed in his own end zone). Baugh and Washington head coach Dudley DeGroot argued their case, but it was the correct call

Other Milestones of 1945

✔ The Hockey Hall of Fame opened in Toronto, Ontario. Howie Morenz was one of nine players elected as the Hall's first class of inductees. Since then, more than 340 other hockey greats from on and off the ice have been inducted. The Hall offers fans awesome displays of hockey memorabilia and trophies.

✔ The NFL's Chicago Cardinals beat the Chicago Bears 16–7 on October 14, ending their record 29-game losing streak. The Cardinals then promptly lost their last six games of the season.

✔ University of Michigan football coach Herbert "Fritz" Crisler introduced the platoon system, sending out different squads to play offense and defense against Army.

✔ The Rockford Peaches won the championship of the All-American Girls Baseball League, which had switched from softball this season.

Superstar Wayne Gretzky at the Hockey Hall of Fame

according to the NFL rulebook of the day. The Rams went up 2–0.

Early in the second quarter, DeGroot took Baugh out of the game. The great passer's injuries had gotten worse, and he had completed just one of six passes.

Baugh's replacement, Frank Filchock, was no slouch. He led the NFL in completions (84) and touchdown passes (13) in 1944, and he quickly connected with Steve Bagarus for a touchdown. Waterfield responded with a 37-yard touchdown pass to end Jim Benton. The teams swapped scoring passes in the third quarter. Waterfield missed an extra point, but his team maintained a tight 15–14 lead.

And that's how it ended. The Redskins twice got close enough for Joe "Hot Toe" Aguirre to attempt fourth-quarter field goals, but even his toes had gone cold. Cleveland won its first championship. A month later, the NFL rule book was revised. In the future, any pass that hit the goal post would be ruled incomplete.

1946

Jurassic Shaq

Basketball's popularity had grown substantially during the war, because it required few players and little equipment. When the conflict ended, two professional basketball leagues began vying for the public's attention—and money. The National Basketball League (NBL) had quietly operated in the Midwest for several years. It was now challenged by the Basketball Association of America (BAA), with teams in Boston, Chicago, Cleveland, Detroit, New York, Philadelphia, Pittsburgh, Providence, St. Louis, Toronto, and Washington, D.C.

Goaded by the competition, the NBL made headlines when the Chicago Gears signed George Mikan (see page 83), the All-America center, for $60,000 over five years. It was considered an absurdly generous contract; the Gears were defunct in a year.

A Moment's Hesitation

For baseball fans, the 1946 season must have seemed like waking from a bad dream. The familiar players who had steadily been drafted away from the game were back, most of them taking their old spots in the lineup. The Boston Red Sox were thrilled to get reacquainted with Ted Williams, slick-fielding second baseman Bobby Doerr, shortstop Johnny Pesky (born John Paveskovich, he had once shined Doerr's shoes as a clubhouse boy in Portland, Oregon), and center fielder Dom DiMaggio (Joe's younger brother).

Williams pounded American League pitching for a .342 batting average and 38 home runs. Apparently he was unaffected by the rise of the "Boudreau Shift." Conceived by Cleveland Indians manager Lou Boudreau during a doubleheader in which Williams drove in 11 runs, it shifted everyone but the left fielder to the right side of second base—where Williams most often hit the ball. But it didn't stop Williams.

Pesky chipped in with a league-best 208 hits, and asthmatic pitcher David "Boo" Ferriss won 25 games. The Red Sox won the pennant by 12 games.

Things were much tighter in the National League, where the St. Louis Cardinals and Brooklyn Dodgers finished tied at 96 wins, necessitating the first playoff in Major League Baseball history. The Cardinals, who were powered by Stan

Almost Unstoppable *Running back Marion Motley (page 64) was among the first African Americans in the NFL, as well as one of the greatest players of all time.*

Musial (.365, 228 hits) and Enos Slaughter (130 RBI), won consecutive games against Brooklyn and claimed their fourth pennant in five years (the first under new manager Eddie Dyer).

The World Series in October was a classic. The two featured hitters fell flat—Musial batted .222, Williams only .200 with one RBI—but the evenly matched teams traded wins and were tied after six games.

St. Louis took a 3–1 lead in game seven, but DiMaggio tied it up with a two-run double off screwball pitcher Harry

1946

Breechen, who had come on in relief after winning game six. In the top of the eighth inning, Slaughter faced off against Red Sox reliever Bob Klinger. Slaughter's availability had been in doubt, since he was hit by a pitch on the right elbow in game five. Klinger, because of an illness in his family, was pitching for the first time in 27 days. Slaughter won this confrontation with a single.

After outs by third baseman Whitey Kurowski and catcher Del Rice, outfielder Harry Walker singled to left-center field. Slaughter was running on the pitch, and when center fielder Leon Culbertson came up with the ball, Slaughter kept running . . . and running.

Pesky caught the outfield throw and turned to face home plate, but hesitated before throwing the ball home. His throw

went 10 feet up the first base line, and Slaughter scored the go-ahead run.

"You could almost say it was a dumb play that worked," catcher Joe Garagiola said about Slaughter's sprint. "You know the difference between dumb and smart—the word 'safe.'"

Breechen retired the Red Sox in order in the top of the ninth inning to win his third game of the World Series. The Cardinals were champions.

A Black-and-White Plan

When Branch Rickey bought into the Brooklyn Dodgers in 1945, his main goals were to field a competitive team and to make some money. But he also had a private agenda. He wanted to break the silent but powerful color barrier that had kept African Americans out of Major League Baseball since the turn of the century.

Rickey wasn't the only man with such ideas. Bill Veeck, Jr. had planned to buy the Philadelphia Phillies and fill the roster with black players in 1943, but had been blocked by Kenesaw Mountain Landis, Major League Baseball's segregationist commissioner.

In 1945, *People's Voice* sportswriter Joe Bostic ambushed Rickey, demanding a tryout for two black players he had escorted to the Dodgers' training camp. A week after that, the Boston Red Sox—pressured by a city councilman and another writer—gave auditions to three Negro League players. None of the athletes ever heard from the teams.

But Rickey, respected throughout the major leagues, was in a unique position to

Super Shortstop *St. Louis Cardinals shortstop Lou Boudreau, who doubled as the team's manager during the 1946 championship season, used this glove during his Hall-of-Fame career.*

see it through, and he had tacit support from Happy Chandler, the new baseball commissioner (see page 54). All Rickey needed was the perfect player.

The Dodgers' boss knew that whomever he selected would be subjected to blinding public scrutiny and abuse on and off the field. Many players and countless fans would be rooting for him to fail. Rickey needed someone above reproach. He chose Jackie Robinson (1919–1972), shortstop for the Kansas City Monarchs of the Negro American League.

The grandson of a slave, raised by a single mother in Pasadena, California, Robinson had been one of the nation's top collegiate athletes, becoming UCLA's first four-letter man and excelling at baseball, football, basketball, and track. (He also won the Pacific Coast intercollegiate golf title.) He also had served in the Army, where he was court-martialed, then acquitted, for challenging the segregation of an Army bus at Fort Hood, Texas. Most agreed that Robinson was not the best player in the Negro Leagues. But he was very good, he didn't smoke or drink, and he was a true soldier in the war against the segregation laws that kept the United States divided by race.

As the story goes, Rickey interviewed Robinson, informed him of the plan, then proceeded to launch an increasingly vile series of racial taunts, testing the player's resolve. As Robinson wrote in his autobiography, "'Mr. Rickey,' I asked, 'are you looking for a Negro who is afraid to fight back?' I never will forget the way he exploded. 'Robinson,' he said, 'I am looking for a ball player with guts enough not to fight back.'"

Man with a Plan *Branch Rickey changed the face of baseball—and America—by signing Jackie Robinson.*

Robinson swore he could handle the job, and he was soon playing for the Dodgers' AAA team in Montreal. He led the International League with a .349 batting average and took the Royals to the 1946 minor league title, scoring the deciding run in the final game against Louisville of the American Association. Robinson had started down the road, but no one was sure where it would lead.

They Got a Football

Pro football once seemed seedy and decidedly less appealing than the college game. Lately, though, it was attracting attention—and paying customers—and some wanted to get into the fraternity. Among them were actor Don

1946

Ameche, oilman James Brueil, and lumber baron Anthony Morabito.

When the NFL shut the door on them, these three men met with other financial bigwigs at a meeting organized by Arch Ward (1896–1955), sports editor of the *Chicago Tribune*, on June 4, 1944. They came away with plans for a rival league, the All-America Football Conference (AAFC).

In addition to the teams controlled by Ameche in Los Angeles (the ownership group included movie mogul Louis B. Mayer), Brueil in Buffalo, New York, and Morabito in San Francisco, the original AAFC included teams in Cleveland, New York City, Chicago, Brooklyn, and Miami.

Desperate for publicity, the new league named Jim Crowley—like NFL boss Elmer Layden, one of the legendary Four Horsemen of Notre Dame (a group of four players given that famous nickname as collegians)—as its commissioner, and baseball legend Lou Gehrig's widow, Eleanor, as the league's secretary and treasurer.

The AAFC received some bulletin-board material (that is, quotes in the newspaper that would serve to enrage or inspire an opponent) in August 1945, when Layden suggested the AAFC "first get a ball, then make a schedule, and then play a game." Miffed AAFC officials shortened the phrase to "tell them to get a ball first," and repeated it often.

By 1946, the new league had plenty of on-field talent, including more than 100 players with NFL experience, and 40 of the 66 College All-Stars of 1945 (this was a postseason team named by the Associated Press until 1976).

The AAFC's inaugural game was on September 6. More than 60,000 fans came to Cleveland Municipal Stadium to see the Browns host the ill-fated Miami Seahawks. The final score—a 44–0 whipping by the Browns—was a sign of events to come. Harvey Hester's Seahawks, stocked exclusively with Southern boys, went 3–11, wound up $80,000 in debt, and were booted from the league.

The Browns, on the other hand, were a raging success on and off the field. Coached by the brilliant Paul Brown (1908–1991), and loaded with stars such as future Hall-of-Fame quarterback Otto Graham (b.1921) and ends Dante Lavelli and Mac Speedie, they went 12–2 and beat the New York Yankees (named for the baseball team) in the first AAFC Championship Game.

Much Ado About Nothing–Nothing

The University of Notre Dame's football team won the national championship in 1943. But when coach Frank Leahy joined the Navy soon after, the team quickly declined. As teams reassembled in 1946, the Fighting Irish of Notre Dame stocked up again. Star quarterback Johnny Lujack joined returning starters such as halfback Terry Brennan, transfers like big tackle George Connor (who came from Holy Cross College), and blue-chip freshman recruits such as end Leon Hart.

The result was fearsome. Thirteen Notre Dame players rushed for more than 100 yards, although none had more than Emil Sitko's 346. The defense held all

Head Man *Coach Frank Leahy (center) sits with his new 1946 Notre Dame team.*

nine of its opponents to six points or less. In one stretch the Fighting Irish shut out four consecutive opponents.

Notre Dame was coached by the quirky Leahy (1908–1973), a perfectionist who constantly exhorted his players to fight for Our Lady—the Virgin Mary, whom he was certain watched over the Catholic college.

As the Fighting Irish churned through the 1946 schedule, it didn't require advanced calculus to pinpoint the big game. Army's Black Knights had won their last 25 games, and had whipped the Fighting Irish 59–0 in 1944 and 48–0 in 1945.

When the nation's top-ranked teams met on November 9, more than 74,000 fans—including Generals Dwight D. Eisenhower and Omar Bradley—filled New York's Yankee Stadium to the bursting point. The game had been sold out for

months, and scalpers were getting $200 a ticket. That was a month's pay for many Americans at the time.

Leahy had been in the Navy during those two Army whippings, but that did not lessen his desire for revenge. During the week's practice before the game, Leahy had his men chanting, "59 and 48, this is the year we retaliate."

The action was as furious as most had hoped. But the defenses completely dominated the day. Notre Dame mounted the only sustained drive of the game, marching 85 yards to Army's three-yard line. But the Black Knights' defense held there, and Army took over on downs.

As for the Fighting Irish defense, Army ended up with great field position after several intercepted passes and fumble recoveries, but could not take advantage. The closest Army got was the Notre

Little Big Man

When Ben Hogan (1912–1992) was nine years old, his blacksmith father committed suicide. Hogan began working as a caddy at a Fort Worth, Texas, golf club at the age of 12, and he turned pro at 17.

Hogan, who was forced to grow up in a hurry, burned with an intensity rarely seen on the golf course. He often practiced for eight hours a day, learning to shoot long drives and to use every club in the golf bag with precision.

"I can't explain it, because I'm not a psychologist," his contemporary and fellow golfer, Byron Nelson, said. "But players were genuinely afraid of him, afraid of playing with him. He wasn't ugly to them, but there was something about that cold stare of his."

Hogan, who stood just 5-foot-9, did not really heat up until 1946, when he returned from service in the U.S. Army Air Corps at the age of 34. He won the PGA tournament that year, beginning a streak of nine victories in 16 majors.

Hogan didn't slow down for 15 years. From 1946 through 1960, he never finished out of the top 10 in a major tournament in the United States. In 1953 he became the first golfer to win three of four majors in one year. Only Tiger Woods has matched that feat.

Dame 15-yard line. Glenn Davis and Doc Blanchard combined for a paltry 80 yards on 25 carries. Notre Dame's Lujack completed only six of 17 passes for 52 yards. All three players finished among the top four in Heisman voting that year.

In the end, it was one of the most memorable games of the decade. But neither team could get on the scoreboard, and the game ended in a 0–0 tie.

After the standoff with Army, Notre Dame won 21 straight games. The Irish also won the 1946 national championship, the first of three in just four seasons. (The freshmen who entered in 1946 graduated with a sparkling 36–0–2 record.)

Unbowed by any opponent, the Irish could be deterred only by their own administration. School officials, concerned that football was outpacing the importance paid to academics, cut the number of scholarships in half, and the team fell to 4–4–1 in 1950.

The College Football End-Around

Football players who had left college to fight in the war regained their eligibility upon return, plus funds for college from the GI Bill—but nothing said they had to play for their old schools. The resulting scramble excited coaches and angered critics across America.

In the October 14 issue of *Time* magazine, American University President Paul F. Douglas said, "Post-war college football has no more relation to education than bullfighting to agriculture. . . . A football player is nothing more than a human slave caught in the biggest black market operation in . . . education."

The *Saturday Evening Post* did its own story, referring to "football's black market." The magazine pointed to Shorty McWilliams, who had started for Army before transferring to Mississippi State University. An MSU booster, it was alleged, offered McWilliams $15,000 in

Pacific Time

The West Coast had no professional sports teams before the end of World War II. Many had discussed it. Before the 1940 Major League Baseball season, for example, a group of West Coast businessmen put together $5 million to entice a team. The St. Louis Browns and Philadelphia Phillies both said no. The main reason was long-distance travel. It had once been almost impossible. Now it was merely expensive.

The AAFC broke the drought. The new football league placed teams in San Francisco (the 49ers) and Los Angeles (the Dons).

The NFL was not to be outdone. Cleveland Rams owner Dan Reeves got permission to move his team. Just weeks after winning the NFL Championship Game against the Washington Redskins, the Rams moved to Los Angeles in January 1946.

Suddenly, the biggest city in the West had not one, but two professional football teams.

---

cash, a car, a $300-a-week summer job, and a permanent job after graduation. Oklahoma A&M officials charged that its rival, the University of Oklahoma, spent $200,000 to buy its football team, and that individual players were receiving as much as $10,000 to suit up.

For better or worse, the NCAA did nothing at all.

Battle of the Military

After its epic scoreless tie with Notre Dame, Army managed to hang on to the nation's number-one ranking. Three weeks later, on November 30, the Black Knights took the field for their last game of the season, against Navy, in front of approximately 100,000 fans at Philadelphia's Municipal Stadium.

Army had arranged to bring its entire cadet corps down from West Point in a 36-car train. But a strike by the United Mine Workers resulted in a coal shortage. The cadets arrived in 50 buses instead.

Navy had won its first game of the 1946 season, then dropped seven straight as injuries struck down its five best backs. The Navy Midshipmen began the Army game as 28-point underdogs, and were down 21–6 at halftime. But Army started to look vulnerable in the second half. Navy marched 78 yards for a third-quarter touchdown and, after stopping the Black Knights on fourth-and-goal, added another score on a pass from Bill Earl to Leon Bramlett at the start of the fourth quarter. Unfortunately, Navy missed all three of its extra points; instead of a 21–21 tie, the Midshipmen trailed 21–18.

After several changes of possession, Navy got the ball with seven and a half minutes remaining. As the clock wound down and the afternoon light grew dim, the team started to drive. On fourth down from the Army 23-yard line, fullback Lynn Chewning broke away for a twisting 20-yard run, leaving Navy at first-and-goal at the three-yard line.

One minute, 23 seconds remained. The crowd surged out of the stands and gathered along the sidelines, with most voices cheering for the Navy underdogs. Chewning ran right, then left, and

1946

was stopped twice for no gain. On third down, Navy hesitated and was hit with a delay-of-game penalty, moving the line of scrimmage back to the eight-yard line. Another run gained four yards. The Navy Midshipmen desperately tried to get in position for a field-goal attempt, but the gun sounded, ending the game and their dreams of an upset.

Navy's one consolation: It had knocked Army from its top spot in the polls. After this game, Notre Dame became number one. Army would never again be the college football powerhouse it was in 1944–45.

MARION MOTLEY

An All-Time Great *This football card honors the Pro Football Hall of Fame induction for Marion Motley.*

The Quiet Pioneers

Jackie Robinson was still a year away from integrating Major League Baseball. With little fanfare, four black men shattered a barrier that had cast a shadow over pro football since 1933. The Los Angeles Rams signed halfbacks Kenny Washington and Woody Strode—both of whom had played with Jackie Robinson at UCLA—and the AAFC's Cleveland Browns signed guard Bill Willis and fullback Marion Motley (1920–1999).

Washington, hobbled by bad knees, played three seasons in Los Angeles; Strode played only one. But Willis and Motley later made the jump to the NFL, and both ended up in the Pro Football Hall of Fame. Before getting that far, they had to weather the hatred and racism that would define Robinson's early career.

"We went down to play Miami one time in 1946, and they told Paul that the two black guys had to stay at a different hotel," Browns quarterback Otto Graham recalled. "Paul said, 'Okay, let's all go.' The whole team was going to go, but then the hotel changed its mind and let us stay. That stuff went on all the time."

He Got His Title

By 1946, Sugar Ray Robinson had just about everything a boxer could ask for: good health, a nearly spotless record, and the respect of the boxing world. About the only thing he lacked was a championship belt. He had come close on numerous times, but had never won the key fights that would have given him the coveted title belt (a trophy traditionally

Other Milestones of 1946

✔ Assault, ridden by jockey by Walter Mehrtens, won horse racing's Triple Crown.

✔ Lloyd Mangrum won the U.S. Open golf tournament in June, edging Byron Nelson and Vic Ghezzi by a stroke after all three had tied in the first playoff round.

✔ The New York Yankees became the first baseball team to travel exclusively by air, signing a contract with United Air Lines.

✔ Bert Bell replaced Elmer Layden as the commissioner of the NFL.

✔ After spending three years in the military, the Pittsburgh Steelers' "Bullet" Bill Dudley returned to lead the NFL in rushing (604 yards), interceptions (10), and punt returns (385 yards).

Alice Coachman

✔ Amos Alonzo Stagg completed his final year as a college football coach. He coached a record 57 seasons, the last 14 at University of the Pacific.

✔ Alice Coachman became the first black woman to join the United States All-American track and field team.

✔ The Ladies Professional Golf Association (LPGA) was formed.

✔ Hockey legend Gordie Howe (b.1928) played the first of his 32 seasons as a pro, starting out with the Detroit Red Wings.

✔ The automatic pinspotter, which reset knocked-down bowling pins mechanically, made its debut in bowling, which soon became America's top participation sport. Previously, the pins had to be reset by hand.

awarded to the champion of a particular weight class.)

That finally changed on December 20, when Robinson outboxed Tommy Bell in a 15-round decision to claim the vacant welterweight title. Over the next four years Robinson beat every man he faced, including future welterweight champion Kid Gavilan (twice) and future middleweight champ Bobo Olson.

1947

The Fancy Pants Triumph

Boston is not really a big college basketball town. It certainly wasn't back in 1947. In those days, the Boston Bruins hockey and Boston Red Sox baseball teams got all the attention. So the popularity of the 1946–47 College of the Holy Cross basketball team came as something of a surprise. The team had a deft shooter in All-American George Kafton, and enough tricky ball handlers to make frustrated opponents label their style "fancy pants." Holy Cross went 24–3, then triumphed 58–47 over University of Oklahoma in the NCAA tournament title game in March.

The fanciest of the fancy-pants was an innovative and creative ballhandler named Bob Cousy (b.1928). The future Basketball Hall of Famer was a freshman that season and used a dazzling blend of behind-the-back dribbling and no-look passes to give the school its only national title. Though Holy Cross was great for the remainder of his time there, the school was not NCAA champ again. But he would return to the top of the basketball world numerous times in his great career with another Boston hoops team—the Celtics.

Everything Is Changed

In the winter of 1947, Brooklyn Dodgers president Branch Rickey ordered his AAA team manager to move Jackie Robinson from second base to first. Rickey then had his major league manager, Leo Durocher, tell a few sportswriters that a solid first baseman was all Brooklyn needed to win the pennant.

Rickey's intentions were clear. He was ready to make Robinson the major leagues' first African-American player in 50 years. Immediately, several Dodgers, led by pitcher Hugh Casey, threatened to quit if they had to play with a black man. Rickey said he would accept their resignations, and they backed off.

On April 15, Robinson started for the Dodgers at first base, and forever changed the game of baseball; some would say he also forever changed America.

The near-mutiny on the Dodgers was just the beginning. Playing the Philadelphia Phillies in late April, Robinson was taunted viciously by Ben Chapman, the Phillies' Alabama-born manager. "At no time in my life have I heard racial venom and dugout abuse to match the abuse that Ben sprayed on Robinson that

Historic Moment *African-American first baseman Jackie Robinson was part of the Dodgers' starting infield on April 15, 1947.*

night," sportswriter Harold Parrott noted. "Chapman mentioned. . .the repulsive sores and diseases he said Robinson's teammates would become infected with if they touched the towels or the combs he used."

Robinson kept his emotions hidden, although friends knew he could have a fiery temper. Chapman's behavior only succeeded gaining support for Robinson. Fans wrote letters of protest to Commissioner Happy Chandler, and newsman Walter Winchell criticized the Phillies' manager on the radio. Chapman and Robinson soon posed for a photo together, each smiling through clenched teeth.

1947

Then, on May 9, the *New York Herald-Tribune* wrote of an alleged plot by members of the St. Louis Cardinals to strike rather than play against a black man. According to the newspaper, National League president Ford Frick (1894–1978) said anyone who pulled such a stunt would be banned from baseball. Cardinals players categorically denied the report.

Robinson may have been making civil rights history in 1947. But his presence had another effect, certainly anticipated by Rickey—who never stopped being a businessman. The rookie was generating impressive ticket sales across the league. At Philadelphia and Cincinnati in May, his visits set attendance records.

Robinson's appeal was twofold. Many white fans came to see him out of a sense of novelty. And blacks turned out in huge

numbers to pay homage to their instant hero. Thousands of black fans stood to applaud Robinson at every Dodgers' road game. A "Jackie Robinson Special" train ran all the way from Norfolk, Virginia, to Cincinnati for Dodgers–Reds games, loading up fans along the way.

"The noble experiment had less to do with brotherhood than it had to do with business," University of California at Berkeley sociologist Harry Edwards once reflected. "Finally it became clear there was all this Negro talent out there, all these Negro fans."

As African Americans poured into National League stadiums, they changed the dynamic of spectator sports in America. This was the first time some whites and blacks found themselves in a place where they could mingle, and many whites were surprised to discover how much they and the black fans had in common.

Robinson's season certainly had its ugly moments, but it was largely a success. He scored 125 runs and won the first balloting for Rookie of the Year, for both leagues combined.

In a wider sense, sports had brought the races together in a way that no amount of legislation or court decisions could.

As baseball writer Roger Kahn wrote, "By applauding Robinson, a man did not feel that he was taking a stand on school integration or on open housing. But for an instant he had accepted Robinson simply as a hometown ball player. To disregard color, even for an instant, is to step away from old prejudices, the old hatred. That is not a path on which many double back."

Still, Robinson's presence didn't exactly open the floodgates of integration

Instant Hero *Young fans, black and white, clamored for Robinson's autograph at Ebbets Field in Brooklyn. While many fans treated him as a hero, others did not give him such a warm reception.*

Satchel Paige

The Negro Leagues boasted some of the finest athletes and ballplayers in America. They played a brand of baseball that valued speed, guile, and defense, along with solid pitching and hitting. In competition for fans with Major League Baseball, it was also open to promoting characters with personality. No man combined both stunning talent with showmanship like Leroy "Satchel" Paige (1906–1982), the one-of-a-kind pitcher who was part athlete, part entertainer.

Born in a Mobile, Alabama, ghetto, the seventh of 11 children, he picked up his nickname while carrying bags at the train station at the age of seven. He was pitching for the local Mobile Tigers at the age of 18, and by 1930 he was legendary throughout the South.

Paige was at his best while throwing for the Kansas City Monarchs of the Negro American League, leading them to four straight pennants. Even then, he pitched for other teams as needed. His appearances were legendary. He would call in the outfielders, stand alone on the field, and strike out the side. Here's one description of a game in Newark, Ohio, written by Tristam Potter Coffin:

> "Between innings, Paige sat in a rocking chair and sipped from a black bottle. He used all his eccentric pitches, throwing overhand, sidearm, underhand; showed the batters the hesitation pitch, the two-hump blooper, the fastballs Long Tom and Little Tom."

Satchel Paige

Paige finally got to play in the newly integrated major leagues in 1948. He won six and lost one for the Cleveland Browns as a 42-year-old, aiding the team's American League title run. He returned to pitch in 103 games for the Browns in 1952–53, although by then he was approaching 50. And he was barnstorming (playing exhibition games)—and still attracting huge crowds—long after that.

in Major League Baseball, or in the wider American society. The Dodgers signed several Negro League stars in the next two years, including Roy Campanella and Don Newcombe, and Cleveland's Larry Doby broke the American League color line in 1948. But many teams remained all-white for years. The final team to integrate was the Red Sox, in 1959.

Here Comes Cookie

The 1947 World Series in October featured baseball's most popular player, the New York Yankees' Joe DiMaggio, and its man of the hour, the Brooklyn Dodgers' Jackie Robinson. But the wild six-game shootout wound up being dominated by virtual no-names.

Babe and Bush

The University of California at Berkeley beat Yale University in baseball's first College World Series in June. Yale's first baseman was future President George Herbert Walker Bush (b.1924). At the event, Bush (center, in cap) greeted visiting baseball legend Babe Ruth.

The Yankees came out swinging and won the first two games. Game two was notable primarily for the fielding adventures of Dodgers center fielder Pete Reiser, who fell down chasing one triple, lost two others in confusion, let a pop fly fall in front of him for a double, and misplayed a single. Game three was just as sloppy. After eight pitchers and three hours, five minutes of play (it was the longest World Series game to that time), the Dodgers won 9–8.

The next game was the one that left fans in disbelief. Yankees starter Floyd "Bill" Bevens had a fastball like lightning, but his accuracy was always a question. He had foundered to a 7–13 record in 1947. In game four of the Series, he was at his unpredictable best and worst. After eight innings on a cold afternoon

at Ebbets Field, Bevens had surrendered eight walks. He was also three outs away from becoming the first pitcher to throw a no-hitter in a World Series game. The Dodgers had scored once in the fifth inning (on two walks, a bunt, and an infield out), but trailed 2–1 as they came to the plate for their last at-bat in the bottom of the ninth.

Catcher Bruce Edwards drove the ball to the left-field wall for a long first out. Carl Furillo walked. John "Spider" Jorgensen fouled out. Reiser came up as a pinch hitter, but when pinch runner Al Gionfriddo stole second (on a poor throw from the young Yankees' catcher, Yogi Berra), Yankees manager Bucky Harris ordered Reiser walked intentionally. It was Bevens' 10th walk.

Dodgers manager Burt Shotton—the temporary replacement of Leo Durocher, whom Commissioner Happy Chandler had suspended for consorting with gamblers—then turned to Harry "Cookie" Lavagetto to pinch hit. Lavagetto was a popular veteran who had inspired the chant, "Lookie, lookie, lookie, here comes Cookie." But in 1947 he hit .261 in only 69 at-bats.

With the count no balls and one strike, Lavagetto drilled the ball past right-fielder Tommy Henrich. Gionfriddo scored, and so did pinch runner Eddie Miksis. Bevens lost the game, the no-hitter, and the Series lead on one pitch.

There was more excitement in the Series. After the Yankees won another one, game six wound up being even longer, at three hours, 19 minutes. With two Yankees on base and the Dodgers leading 8–5 in the sixth inning, DiMaggio hit the ball straight at the 415-foot sign in left-center field at Yankee Stadium. It was just over the wall—and then it was in the glove of Gionfriddo, who somehow managed to cover a huge distance and make a sweet backhanded catch while leaning into the bullpen. The Yankees lost.

But the Yanks won game seven behind relief pitcher Joe Page, who shut down the Dodgers over the final five innings, and Henrich, who delivered his third game-winning hit of the Series.

The strangest twist to this wacky Series was that the three top performers—Bevens, Lavagetto, and Gionfriddo—were all playing their last professional games.

Chicago Dreaming

The Chicago Bears had captured six NFL titles since 1925. In that same 22-year period, the Bears' neighbors, the Cardinals, had gone dry. The Cardinals' fortunes began to change in 1946, though, when fullback Pat Harder and right halfback Elmer Angsman joined quarterback Paul Christman in the backfield.

The final piece of the puzzle was Charley Trippi, the Heisman Trophy runner-up from the University of Georgia. And he didn't come cheap. Cardinals owner Charles Bidwill found himself in a bidding war with Dan Topping, who owned the AAFC's New York Yankees, and wound up signing Trippi to a princely four-year, $100,000 contract—the largest football contract ever at the time.

Trippi took his spot at left halfback in the Cardinals' T formation, and collectively the four men became known as the "Dream Backfield." Finally the South Siders had something to cheer about as their Cardinals won the Western Division and hosted the Philadelphia Eagles in the

A New Spin

At Yale University, one of the oldest student traditions was to take the sloped pie tins of a local bakery—the Frisbie Pie Company of Bridgeport, Connecticut—and toss them back and forth. In 1947, two enterprising Californians took the game to a higher level.

Fred Morrison and Warren Francioni made a flying disk of plastic and called it the Frisbee. The toy caught on quickly, and the name was patented by the Wham-O Manufacturing Company. A half-century later, Frisbee-catching dogs were a staple of football halftime entertainment.

An old Frisbie pie tin (right) and a modern Frisbee.

1947

NFL Championship Game at Chicago's Comiskey Park on December 28.

The Dream Backfield turned out to be a pure nightmare for the Eagles. The Cardinals scored on several big plays: Trippi ran 44 yards for one touchdown and returned a punt 75 yards for another score, breaking five tackles along the way. Angsman ran for a pair of 70-yard touchdowns, and the Cardinals prevailed 28–21. (The Cardinals later moved to St. Louis and then to their current home in Arizona.)

Still the Champ *Joe Louis continued his remarkable reign as the heavyweight champion, holding on to the title after two memorable 1948 bouts with the hard-hitting Jersey Joe Walcott.*

Still the Best . . . Maybe

One thing World War II hadn't been able to change was that Joe Louis was still the heavyweight champion. He had started to slip, but no one else was good enough to take away his belt.

On December 5, Louis faced Jersey Joe Walcott (1914–1994), a veteran boxer who had been fighting for years with mixed results. Bookmakers put Walcott's odds at 15–to–1. But he stunned the New York crowd, knocking down the champion in the first and fourth rounds and outboxing him for much of the fight.

Louis exited the ring after the last round, apparently figuring he had lost. But two of three judges gave the decision to the champ, who apologized to Walcott.

The rematch came on June 25, 1948, and again Walcott tormented Louis with his quick moves. This time, there was no need for a judges' decision. Louis awoke to batter his foe in the 10th round, then knock him out in the 11th round. But these victories, far from being sweet, only served to show how far Louis had fallen since his glory days.

The Birth of Speed

Bill France (1909–1992) spent the war at the Daytona Beach Boat Works. When the conflict ended, he returned to his first love—building and racing cars, primarily on the sand.

Big Bill (as the 6-foot-5 France was called) loved racing and was a regular on the sand tracks of Florida's east coast, but he saw that an average driver in an expensive car could usually beat a good

Other Milestones of 1947

✔ The Philadelphia Warriors won the first championship of the Basketball Association of America, four games to one over the Chicago Stags, in March.

✔ Fans begin to choose the starting lineups for the Major League Baseball All-Star Game with a mail-in ballot.

✔ The first Little League World Series was held in Williamsport, Pennsylvania, in August. A local team, Maynard Little League, won the tournament.

Warriors star Joe Fulks

✔ Althea Gibson won the first of 10 consecutive American Tennis Association season titles. The ATA put on a series of amateur tennis tournaments for African-American players.

✔ The annual National Hockey League All-Star Game was played for the first time on October 13,

before the start of the season. In 1962, it moved to its current spot in mid-season. Stars from the two NHL conferences meet (though some recent games have pitted North American versus European players instead).

✔ Former New York Giants outfielder Danny Gardella sued Major League Baseball for $350,000, saying the major leagues' reserve clause is a violation of national antitrust laws. The reserve clause bound players to the team that first signed them. Gardella eventually settled for $60,000, and the reserve clause was not challenged successfully until the 1970s.

✔ Boston Red Sox outfielder Ted Williams won his second Triple Crown, winning A.L. titles in home runs, RBI, and batting.

driver in a lesser car. His dream was to create an organization in which all the cars operated within the same guidelines—"stock cars," so to speak.

On December 14, France assembled 25 men at the Streamline Hotel in Daytona Beach, Florida. He talked about codified rules and a points system that would crown a national champion. He stressed the importance of clean, brightly painted cars. "Nothing stands still in the world," Big Bill said. "Things get better or worse, bigger or smaller."

It was mechanic Red Vogt who came up with the name for the group that everyone liked: the National Association

for Stock Car Auto Racing—better known today as NASCAR.

On February 15, 1948, six days before incorporating NASCAR, France held the first race on Daytona Beach. The winner was Red Byron. He was driving what was called a "modified" car. NASCAR had to wait until 1949 for true stock cars; the Detroit auto plants were still backed up with new-car orders, having ceased commercial production during the war.

To this day, control of NASCAR, now one of the biggest sports in the nation, remains in the France family. Bill France Jr., took over in 1972; his son Brian France succeeded Mike Helton in 2003.

1948

Let the Games Return

How do you know if things are back to normal? When the Olympics return. After World War II caused the cancellation of the Games in 1940 and 1944, both Winter and Summer Games returned in 1948. The Winter Games were held in February in St. Moritz, Switzerland, in February. The ski-resort town had been practically untouched by the war, and 28 nations sent 706 athletes to the Games.

The United States made a decent showing in the Winter Olympics, ranking fourth overall with 19 medals and tying for third with three golds.

Skier Gretchen Fraser of Vancouver, Washington, clocked the fastest time in the first run of the women's slalom skiing event. But as she prepared to lead off the second round, the telephone timing system that connected the top of the hill with the bottom stopped working. Fraser waited 17 minutes in the chute, but turned in a strong time anyway and won the gold. She also took silver in the alpine combined event.

The U.S. four-man bobsled team—a burly group from Lake Placid, New York, who averaged 224 1/2 pounds—also over-

came technical difficulties before finishing first. Competition was halted in the middle of the second round when a water pipe burst and flooded the bobsled run.

For John Heaton, the hurdle wasn't technology but time. He won consecutive silver medals in the skeleton (a type of sledding performed headfirst and face-down) 20 years apart. He was 19 years old the first time, 39 years old in 1948.

Resolute as a Button

Dick Button (b.1929) had been a rolypoly child, 5-foot-2 and 162 pounds at the age of 12. Dismissed by a figure skating coach, he worked hard to lose weight and hone his skills on the ice. By 1946, Button won the U.S. men's figure skating championship. In 1948, now 18 years old and a freshman at Harvard University, he was the country's best hope to win a gold medal in figure skating—something no American had ever done.

As the leader heading into the final round, Button was faced with a dilemma. He had completed a double axel jump for the first time only three weeks earlier. Should he attempt the flashy move now, or be cautious? Button went for the gusto

Rings Are Back   *Olympic athletes returned after they were interrupted by the war (page 74 and 78).*

and nailed the double. Eight of nine judges gave him their highest score; only one, the Swiss judge, gave the highest score to Swiss skater Hans Gerschwiler. Button went home with the gold medal.

A week after the Olympics, Button won the world championship in Davos, Switzerland. He then launched a tour to show off his athletic style, which was characterized as uniquely American. One of the stops was Prague, Czechoslovakia, which had just fallen to Soviet-backed Communist soldiers. As Button entered the rink, he was greeted with a hail of oranges. "I thought this was the Czech version of an anti-American raspberry, and I threw the first orange off the rink," he said. "However, when others were thrown, I picked one up and noticed the paper in which it was wrapped had some encouraging words written on it: GOOD LUCK, U.S.A. Another said, COME ON, BUTTON!" In the new Cold War world, things were not always what they seemed. Button went on to enjoy a long career as a skating analyst on television.

Tale of the Red Tape

The Olympics are supposed to represent an ideal of human competition, where athletes rise above the petty issues of the day. Alas, politics intrude here as they do elsewhere. When the 1948 Winter Olympics began, two U.S. hockey teams arrived ready to compete. One was sanctioned by the American Hockey Association (AHA), the other by the American Olympic Committee (AOC), whose president, Avery Brundage (1887–1975), accused the AHA of commercialism.

The Swiss Olympic Committee ruled that the AOC team could take part in the opening ceremony, and the AHA team would then play all the games. The International Olympic Committee (IOC) countered by nullifying the entire tournament. The Americans (the AHA team) won by some amazing scores, beating Poland 23–4 and Italy 31–1. In the end, though, the IOC announced it would sanction the tournament only if the AHA team didn't appear in the standings. To this day, it does not.

Major Deals

Hockey was tough business in the 1940s, but it didn't intimidate Conn Smythe (1895–1980), general manager of the Toronto Maple Leafs. Smythe spent 14 months in a German POW camp during World War I, and was wounded while commanding Canada's 30th Antiaircraft Battery in World War II. "World War III," Tim Crothers wrote in the book *Greatest Teams*, "was any game Smythe's Maple Leafs played against the Detroit Red Wings."

Over the decade of the 1940s, the man they called the "Little Major" assembled an indomitable crew. Centers Syl Apps and Ted "Teeder" Kennedy, and chubby goalie Turk Broda had been there for Toronto's championship in 1942. After the war, Smythe added the "Gold Dust Twins"—defensemen Jimmy Thomson and Gus Mortson—and winger Howie Meeker, who nearly had his leg shattered by a grenade during the war.

The Maple Leafs were known for their clutch-and-grab tactics and frequent brawls. But their style triumphed over artistry in the 1947 Stanley Cup finals, when they upset the Montreal Canadiens in six games.

Before the start of the 1947–48 season, Smythe shocked Leafs' fans by trading five of his champions to the Chicago Blackhawks for touted center Max Bentley. Smythe also found another gem that year when he signed 19-year-old defenseman "Bashing" Billy Barilko, who soon was slamming opposing players against the boards around the league.

In the finals in April, Toronto swept past Detroit in four games. The Maple Leafs swept the Red Wings again in 1949, becoming the first NHL team to win three straight Stanley Cups.

A Privilege to Ride

Ask veteran horse racing fans to name the greatest horse of all time, and many of them will say Citation. Certainly, few horses have had a year to match the bay colt's 1948, when he won 19 of his 20 races and finished second in the other. He didn't just win the Triple Crown that year, he ran away with it.

Before the first race of the Crown, the Kentucky Derby, the talk among racing fans was that Coaltown was an even stronger horse than Citation. Certainly, Coaltown was a faster sprinter. The question was, could he keep up his speed over a mile and a quarter? Breeders entered only four other horses, none of them contenders, against the swift duo.

The sun shone as the Derby got under way on May 1, but rain had muddied the track. Coaltown broke strong from the gate, with Citation falling in behind. By the time they reached the far turn, Coaltown was seven lengths ahead. Finally, jockey Eddie Arcaro on Citation made his move. As they came out of the turn and galloped down the stretch, Citation cut the lead to two lengths, then one, then pulled even. Coaltown matched the pace for a few strides, then fell back, and Citation won by three and a half lengths.

Arcaro had his fourth Derby victory—a record—and Citation was on his way to greatness. He entered the Preakness Stakes as a 1–10 sure thing and led from start to finish, winning by five and a half lengths.

"It is a crime to take the money for riding such a horse," Arcaro said after that race. "It is a privilege."

Citation completed his sweep by taking the Belmont Stakes on June 11 by eight lengths. When the colt came to the post for the Pimlico Special that autumn, he couldn't find a challenger. So he breezed around the track solo and picked up $10,000.

After missing a season due to injury, Citation returned to race successfully, and became the first horse to claim more than $1 million in prize money.

Continuing a great decade for memorable horses, Citation was the fourth Triple Crown winner of the 1940s. But no horse would win another until Secretariat in 1973.

A Legend Says Goodbye

On June 13, 1948, Yankee Stadium was silent as fans listened to the man from whom the great sports palace got its nickname: The House that Ruth Built.

Now 53 years old, Babe Ruth was dying. Sick with throat cancer, his once-mighty body was wasting away. On the 25th anniversary of the opening of Yankee Stadium, Ruth returned to say goodbye.

Wearing his famous No. 3 Yankees pinstripe uniform, and using a baseball bat as a cane, he stepped to the microphone and rasped out a few final words. "You know this baseball game of ours comes up from the youth. That means the boys.

The Best Ever? *Citation, ridden by legendary jockey Eddie Arcaro, charges after Coaltown on the way to winning the 1948 Kentucky Derby, the first leg of Citation's Triple Crown.*

1948

And after you've been a boy, and grow up to know how to play ball, then you come to the boys you see representing themselves today in our national pastime."

Then the man who was perhaps most responsible for ensuring baseball's place as the national pastime left the field for the last time. Ruth died two months later. More than 100,000 people filed by his casket as it lay in Yankee Stadium.

Bittersweet Celebration *The Yankees celebrated 25 years of the House That Ruth Built. But when Babe Ruth stepped to the microphone to talk, he was a shell of his former self.*

London Calling

It was a pleasant feeling to have the Summer Olympics in London, which had survived heavy bombing just a few years earlier. But as the Games got under way in July, the hostilities of World War II were too raw—and the global landscape too uncertain—to ignore.

Olympic organizers did not invite Germany, Italy, and Japan, the vanquished Axis powers. And Joseph Stalin's Soviet Union, which quickly changed from America's ally to its chief rival, refused to participate. In June, Soviet troops cut off all surface access to the western sector of the newly divided German city of Berlin. When the Games began a month later, British and American airplanes were flying in food, medical supplies, and fuel to needy Berliners.

Still, a record 59 nations sent athletes to the unseasonably cold and wet British capital to participate in the Games. Without the Soviets there, the United States flattened the competition, winning more gold medals (38) than the next three nations combined (Sweden, France, and Hungary, with a total of 36).

Some of the more notable American winners included:

- Alice Coachman (b.1923) squeaked past Britain's Dorothy Tyler on a technicality in the women's high jump and became the first black woman to win an Olympic gold medal.

- Air Force sergeant Mal Whitfield pulled away in the 800-meter race for the gold. Between 1948 and 1954, Whitfield won 66 of 69 races at that distance.

All-American Boy

By the time Bob Mathias turned 11, he was high-jumping five feet and long-jumping 15. Then he suffered a bout of acute anemia (low iron in his blood), followed in rapid succession by chicken pox, measles, and whooping cough. His father, a Tulare, California, physician who had played football at the University of Oklahoma, helped Mathias regain his strength with vitamins and a healthy diet.

At 17, Mathias entered his first decathlon and scored the highest point total by an American in seven years. Over the next four years, he never lost a decathlon.

After his amazing performance in the 1948 Olympics, Mathias went to Stanford University, where he

Bob Mathias

played football and helped lead the Stanford Indians to the 1952 Rose Bowl. Later that year he claimed gold in the decathlon at the Summer Olympics in Helsinki, Finland, becoming the sport's first two-time Olympic champion.

He never got a shot at a third gold medal. The Amateur Athletic Union declared him a professional after he was paid to star in a biographical movie, *The Bob Mathias Story*.

Mathias proved to be a tireless fighter for amateur athletes. He lobbied for passage of the Amateur Sports Act of 1978—sometimes called the athlete's "Bill of Rights"—and helped guide the establishment of the U.S. Olympic Training Center in Colorado Springs.

- Wilbur Thompson, F. James Delaney, and James Fuchs outdistanced the rest of the world by more than three feet while sweeping the medals in the shotput.

- The U.S. basketball team survived a 59–57 threat from Argentina in an early round (not to mention one comical moment when a Chinese player dribbled between the legs of Bob Kurland, the seven-foot American center, and scored a basket) to win the gold easily. The final score against silver medalist France was 65–21.

- The U.S. women's 4-by-100-meter freestyle relay swimming team came from behind to take the gold over Denmark, after a spectacular anchor swim by Ann Curtis (b.1926).

- Vicki Draves grew up in San Francisco, the child of a Filipino father and an English mother. She became the first female diver to win two gold medals in one Olympics.

- Light-heavyweight lifter Stanley Stanczyk was given credit for a world-record snatch of 132.5 kilograms, only to startle the referee by confessing that his knee had scraped the floor—a disqualification for that lift. Fortunately, Stanczyk's muscles were as well-developed as his sportsmanship. He won the competition by 37.5 kilograms, the widest margin in Olympic history. The silver medalist, American Harold Sakata, later gained fame for his portrayal of Oddjob in the James Bond movie *Goldfinger*.

1948

Decathlon Champ

Late in Bob Mathias' senior year at Tulare (California) High School, his track coach suggested he consider the decathlon, a track and field sport that combines 10 events. Mathias (b.1930) had never done a pole vault or a long jump, thrown a shotput or a javelin, or run a distance race. But he was confident enough to enter an Olympic regional meet three weeks after the decision, and he stunned observers by winning. A couple weeks after that, he claimed first place at the U.S. national meet in Bloomfield, New Jersey, securing a spot on the 1948 Olympic team.

At age 17, Mathias was the youngest athlete in the history of the U.S. track and field team. The veteran decathletes who gathered in London to compete against him were distinctly unimpressed.

The first day of competition (five of 10 events were scheduled), August 5, was dark and wet. After decent performances in the 100 meters and long jump, Mathias surprised himself with a long shotput. But the novice exited the ring from the front, something he now learned was forbidden. This throw was disqualified, and his next throw wasn't as good.

He ran a swift 400 meters, but faltered in the high jump, twice missing at 5-foot-9. Huddled under a blanket,

Athletic Artistry

Pro football was becoming more colorful in the 1940s—in terms of action, at least. When it came to headgear, the NFL was bland and colorless.

That changed in the spring of 1948, when Fred Gehrke of the Los Angeles Rams' showed his drawings of a yellow ram's horn on a blue background to head coach Bob Snyder.

Gehrke was an accomplished artist as well as a halfback (he had been a technical illustrator for Northrop Aircraft during the war), and the coach loved his drawings. So did Rams owner Dan Reeves. Gehrke painted a helmet each night over the next summer—75 total,

all by hand—lining them up in his garage. The Rams paid him $1 per helmet—just enough to cover the cost of paint—and he touched them up every week throughout the 1948 season.

Gehrke got a break the following year, when the Riddell sporting goods company introduced plastic helmets to the NFL, replacing the old leather version. Now the paint could be applied by machine, baking on the design under a layer of translucent plastic.

The Baltimore Colts soon painted a blue horseshoe on their white helmets, and within a decade most of the teams in the league followed suit.

Mathias made a desperate decision. He abandoned the Western roll technique prevalent at the time (in which the athlete throws one leg over the bar and then "rolls" over with the chest facing the ground) and sprinted straight at the bar, then leaped awkwardly. He cleared the barrier, went on to jump 6-foot-1 1/4, and finished in third place.

The second day's weather was even more dismal, with rain and heavy fog delaying the decathlon until the afternoon. After the 100-meter hurdles and the discus, Mathias had claimed the lead.

By the time officials set up the pole vault, it was 9 p.m. The vaulters had to run down a darkened path toward a bar illuminated with flashlights. Mathias, weakened from effort and lack of food (he hadn't eaten since devouring a box lunch), passed up the preliminary jumps. It was a risky strategy, because he'd be penalized if he failed at 10 feet and would almost certainly lose any hope for the gold medal. But he cleared the bar at 11 feet, 5 3/4 inches.

Mathias won the javelin throw and finished the 1,500 meters in 5:11, quick enough to win the decathlon. He was the youngest person to win an Olympic gold medal in track and field.

No Rain in October

The Boston Braves had a pair of dominant pitchers in 1948. Johnny Sain won 24 games, pitched 315 innings, and recorded 28 complete games. Warren Spahn (1921–2003) won 15 games and threw 257 innings (actually an off year for the man who eventually had more wins—

End of an Era *This replica hat celebrates the Birmingham Black Barons, one of the many long-standing Negro League teams that faded in the late 1940s.*

363—than any other left hander in history). Braves' fans knew the recipe for success, and it became a familiar refrain: "Spahn and Sain and pray for rain."

In the World Series in October, Boston met the Cleveland Indians, who had a fine pitching staff of their own, paced by Bob Feller and Bob Lemon. Cleveland's pitchers were just too much for the Braves, who scored one run or less in each of the first four games, before breaking out with 11 runs in game five.

Gene Bearden, a Navy veteran who had aluminum plates in his head and knees because of war wounds, pitched a five-hit shutout for the Indians in game three, then retired the last four Braves in the decisive sixth game. It was Cleveland's first World Series championship since 1920.

Final Innings

Jackie Robinson's arrival in Major League Baseball in 1947 (see page 66) signaled a bittersweet era for African-

1948

American fans. On one hand, black players now got to compete with the best players in the world, make solid money, and get their names in mainstream newspapers. On the other hand, the change spelled doom for the Negro Leagues that had flourished for decades. The point was hammered home in 1948, when the Negro National League ceased operations after the season.

Nobody would have traded the new opportunities for the old way of life, but there was an aura about the Negro Leagues that couldn't be recaptured. The season usually began in February. Teams barnstormed all over the South, often picking up players along the way. "Rarely were we in the same city two days in a row," said Roy Campanella, who starred for the Baltimore Elite Giants before gaining fame with the Brooklyn Dodgers.

The exhausting tours could include three games in a day. The last, called the twilight game, ended when the hitters could no longer see the ball. Barred from white hotels and restaurants, the players and coaches often slept in private homes, or even on team buses.

The Negro Leagues reached their apex during the war. Some 2 million fans attended games in 1942, and the popular East-West All-Star Game attracted 51,000 spectators in Chicago that year. But when Robinson broke the major league color barrier, the end was inevitable. The Negro American League fielded only four teams in 1953, and struggled mightily before giving up for good in 1960.

Ice Festival

Before the Philadelphia Eagles and Chicago Cardinals faced off in the 1948 NFL Championship Game, they had to do a little housekeeping. Players from both teams joined forces to pull a snow-covered tarpaulin off the field at Shibe Park in Philadelphia. A blizzard was raging—but a football game would still be played.

Within 30 minutes, the field was blanketed with snow again. Officials marked the sidelines with ropes tied to stakes, while the stadium lights cast eerie shadows on the great piles of snow. Amazingly, 28,864 people braved the blizzard to watch the game in the stadium.

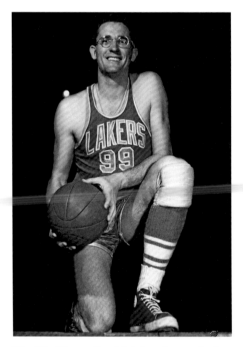

The Big Man *Don't let the glasses fool you. George Mikan was a real basketball pioneer.*

Other Milestones of 1948

✔ The Harlem Globetrotters defeated the Minneapolis Lakers 61–59 in an exhibition game on February 19, before 17,853, the largest crowd ever to see a professional basketball game in Chicago. It was the Globetrotters' sixth game in six nights.

✔ The University of Michigan captured the first NCAA ice hockey championship, beating Dartmouth College in the final round at Colorado Springs in March.

✔ Bowman resumed producing trading cards of sports figures, having curtailed the business during World War II. Topps followed suit in 1951.

Larry Doby

✔ Larry Doby batted .301 in 439 at-bats for the Cleveland Indians. Doby had broken baseball's color line in the American League when he debuted for the Indians on July 5, 1948.

✔ The National Boxing Association announced a new safety program, including a mandatory eight count after knockdowns, and the use of heavily padded eight-ounce gloves.

✔ Forty American rodeo performers— male and female—were escorted to the French border after they were involved in a brawl with spectators and police in Geneva, Switzerland.

The first time the Eagles had the ball, quarterback Tommy Thompson hit end Jack Ferrante with a 65-yard touchdown pass. For a moment, no one noticed the white penalty flag on the white ground; Ferrante had been offside (he moved before the play began). After that, the game settled into a brutal series of inside runs. Chicago quarterback Paul Christman was taken out with an injury. Philadelphia's Steve Van Buren, who rushed for 98 yards, seemed to be the only player able to handle the footing.

Late in the third quarter, Chicago quarterback Ray Mallouf and halfback Elmer Angsman fumbled a handoff, and Philadelphia's Frank Kilroy recovered the ball at the Cardinals' 17-yard line. Four plays later, Van Buren scored from five yards out, giving his team a memorable 7–0 victory, and giving the NFL one of its snowiest days ever.

The First Hoops Giant

Before the 1948–49 season, the Minneapolis Lakers and four other National Basketball League (NBL) teams defected to the Basketball Association of America (BAA). Lakers big man George Mikan averaged 28.3 points in a season when only two other players in the league broke 20. On February 22, 1949, Mikan set a pro scoring record when he poured in 48 points in one game. He later led them to the first BAA title.

Mikan knew how to get position in the paint (the area under the basket), and his shooting touch was excellent. Mikan's greatest asset was his size— 6-foot-10, which was supersized when compared to most centers at the time.

In January 1950, a poll of sportswriters named Mikan the greatest basketball player of the half-century.

1949

A Great Recovery Shot

Events in Texas starting in February of this year proved to be one of the great comeback stories of the decade. On February 2, golfer Ben Hogan and his wife were driving to their home in Texas when a bus suddenly appeared on the road ahead, bearing straight for them. The Hogans' car hit the bus head-on.

Valerie Hogan was fine. But Ben was rushed to a hospital in El Paso, about 100 miles away, where it was reported that he had a double fracture of the pelvis, broken collarbone, fractured rib, broken ankle, and severe internal injuries.

At first no one knew whether he would live. Then there was no guarantee he'd walk again. But Hogan slowly showed signs of improvement, and two weeks after the accident, doctors operated to treat his internal injuries.

Immediately after the operation, the gritty golfer started his rehabilitation program. He began by squeezing a rubber ball to strengthen his fingers, then progressed to stomach exercises designed to mend his abdominal muscles. It wasn't long before he was jogging several miles a day.

Late in 1949, Hogan filed an entry form for the Los Angeles Open, to be held in January 1950. Fans expected him to make only a token appearance. Instead, Hogan played four strong rounds, resting on a chair between shots. He eventually finished second to Sam Snead, losing in a playoff, but proving he was back in the game after only 11 months.

Wildcats Strike

From 1946 through 1954, the University of Kentucky was the king of college basketball. The Wildcats won the NIT title in 1946, fell to the Utah in the NIT final in 1947, and claimed the NCAA crown by topping Baylor University in 1948. Even the 1948 U.S. Olympic team was dominated by Kentucky's "Fabulous Five."

Kentucky was back in the hunt in 1949. Fueled by players such as center Alex Groza, guard Ralph Beard, and forward Wallace Jones, the Wildcats went 29–1 in the regular season and entered the NCAA tournament as the nation's top-ranked team in the first Associated Press college basketball poll. On March 26, the Wildcats defeated Oklahoma State University 46–36 in the final of the

Winning Wildcats *An NCAA title in 1949 was part of an amazing run by Kentucky's basketball team.*

NCAA tournament in Seattle, repeating as champs. The 6-foot-7, 220-pound Groza, rang up 25 points in the final (more than twice as many as any other player), and was the tournament MVP.

Kentucky's shining run of success was dimmed, though, when the team got caught up in the gambling scandal of the early 1950s. Several players were caught helping gamblers win bets.

Our Old Kentucky Coach

The University of Kentucky has won more games, built a higher winning percentage, and made more tournament appearances than any other team in college basketball history. The man who established the foundation—and, indeed, won nearly half of those games—was Adolph Rupp (1901–1977), known as "the man in the brown suit." He coached the Wildcats from 1931 (when he was 30 years old) to 1972 (when he was 71). Along the way, he led Kentucky to four championships in the NCAA tournament and one in the NIT. He also was among the first coaches to develop the fast break.

Rupp ruled his program with an iron fist. He allowed no sloppy attire, card playing, or towel stealing, saying he had no intention of "packing around a bunch of tramps, gamblers, and thieves."

Birth of the NBA

It was clear that America wanted pro basketball in the late 1940s. It was equally clear that the country could not support two separate leagues. So after the 1948–49 season, the Basketball Association of America and the National Basketball League merged into a single entity, the 17-team National Basketball Association (NBA). Its original teams included the Waterloo Hawks, the Sheboygan Redskins, and the Indianapolis Olympians.

Seventeen teams proved to be far too many. The NBA cut down to 10 teams by the 1950–51 season, and down to eight by 1954–55. From that point on, it experienced nothing but gradual growth.

Red's Run

By 1949, race drivers had enough new cars at their disposal that Big Bill Elliott and the folks at NASCAR could call their series Strictly Stock. This is the year many people regard as the true birth of stock car racing.

The first Strictly Stock race was at Charlotte (North Carolina) Speedway—a 3/4-mile dirt oval at the county fairgrounds—on June 19. The winner, Jim Roper, would never be a big name in NASCAR. But the second race, at Daytona, Florida, was captured by Robert "Red" Byron. He had spent two years in military hospitals as doctors attended to his mangled left leg, wounded when his Air Corps bomber was shot down.

Driving a new Oldsmobile with a specially extended clutch pedal, Byron captured the 1949 championship after an eight-race series. He won a second race and collected a whopping total of $5,800 in prize money. His tiny hometown—Talladega, Alabama—would one day become an important center of auto racing.

Net Profits

In the 1940s, tennis remained largely an amateur sport. Professional tours came and went, their membership changing constantly. Many players chose to remain amateurs.

Jack Kramer wasn't the first tennis player to turn pro, but when he organized an extensive national pro circuit in the fall of 1947, it forever changed the structure of the sport. His players included well-known personalities such as Bobby Riggs, Pancho Segura, and Don Budge, and their matches drew big crowds.

The notion got a little bigger on September 20, when star Pancho Gonzalez (1928–1995) signed a one-year pro contract with Riggs, who had become a promoter. The contract guaranteed Gonzalez $60,000 the first year. Kramer and Gonzalez then combined on a tour that began at Madison Square Garden in New York on October 25.

Boomer Sooners

Throughout the 1940s, college football was dominated by teams from the Midwest (Notre Dame, Ohio State, Minnesota) and the military academies (especially Army). But a new power began to emerge in 1948, when Bud Wilkinson's University of Oklahoma Sooners capped a thrilling season with a 14–6 victory over the University of North Carolina in the Sugar Bowl.

Oklahoma was in full bloom in 1949. Wilkinson (1916–1994) was a soft-spoken and professorial young coach with a master's degree in English and experience as a hangar-deck officer on an aircraft carrier during World War II. He coached at Oklahoma for 17 seasons and won three national championships in the 1950s, but many observers feel the 1949 team was Wikinson's best.

The Sooners were hot from the first play of the first game of the season, when the sensational George Thomas fielded the opening kickoff against Boston College and ran it back 95 yards for a touchdown. They won 46–0 and never looked back. By the end of the regular season, Oklahoma was 10–0 and ranked number two in the country, behind Notre Dame.

It was too late for the official rankings (which were settled before the bowls then), but the Sooners' 35–0 drubbing of Louisiana State in the Sugar Bowl on January 1, 1950, made them a popular choice as America's best college team.

Heck on Wheels

Leo Seltzer figured he'd have a box-office smash when he developed roller derby, a sport that involved roller-skating around a circular track and pretending to slam into the opponents. It was a dud for years, however, until Seltzer had a brilliant idea. In 1947 he televised a game in Chicago, and it was a sensation. When people saw roller derby on television, they rushed to see live matches.

By 1949, roller derby (male and female) was being staged in arenas across America, drawing several million paying fans. "The Derby's disruptive effect on the

Speed Tubes *While Red Byron was helping NASCAR get off to a fast start, Indy cars were still going strong. Here's a good look at the type of cars used in the Indy 500, won by Bill Holland.*

1949

household is virtually absolute," *The New York Times* media columnist Jack Gould wrote. "Never before has roller-skating meant so much."

The first World Series of the National Roller Derby filled Madison Square Garden for a week in September, with crowds as large as 13,000. Those numbers grew to 19,000 by 1951. In the mid-1950s, however, television executives flooded the airwaves with games. Roller derby became all too commonplace, and attendance gradually declined.

Peace Time

The competition between the NFL and the AAFC was great for football players, who saw their salaries skyrocket.

Round and Round They Went *The rough sport of roller derby, played on roller skates on wooden indoor ovals, enjoyed enormous popularity in the late 1940s and early 1950s.*

(Before the war, players were getting an average of $150 per game; by 1949 the average minimum salary was $5,000 per year.) It generally piqued fan interest, too. But the four-year league war had devastated the two leagues financially.

Groups representing the rival organizations met in Philadelphia in December of 1948, but talks broke down. So the AAFC forged ahead with the 1949 season, reducing its schedule from 14 games to 12 and merging two teams, Brooklyn and New York. Money was so tight in Chicago that players from the Hornets (a new ownership group had changed the team name from the Rockets) and the visiting Cleveland Browns had to clear the field of snow before their game.

Cleveland dominated the AAFC again. During the four years of league play, the Browns went 47–4–3 and won all four championship games. By 1949, none of the other franchises could come close to Paul Brown's team.

The NFL, for its part, also struggled under the strain of competition. On December 9, the two leagues announced a merger agreement. Under the terms of the pact, the NFL absorbed the Browns, the San Francisco 49ers, and the Baltimore Colts (who had joined the AAFC in 1947 and finished 1–11 in 1949), beginning in 1950. Players from the other four AAFC teams would be dispersed in a draft.

The new body was called the National-American Football League. That tongue-twister of a nickname only lasted about two months, after which it reverted back to the good old NFL. The AAFC would not be the last league to challenge the power of the NFL, however.

Other Milestones of 1949

✔ Bill Lewis, the first black man selected as an All-American in football (during the 1892–93 season), died on January 1 at the age of 80.

✔ Baseball's New York Yankees hired Casey Stengel as manager, ushering in a new winning era for the team.

✔ Marcenia Lyle Alberga was the first woman to play a full season in a men's semipro baseball league.

✔ In July, Major League Baseball owners mandated warning tracks in all stadiums. These strips of dirt still ring the playing surface. Players chasing fly balls can keep their eyes on the ball, knowing that the feel of dirt under their feet will alert them that they are nearing a wall or other barrier.

Casey Stengel

✔ The NFL permanently permitted free substitution, allowing any player to be substituted after each play. Previously, players removed from a game could not return in the same quarter.

✔ George Blanda joined football's Chicago Bears as a rookie. He didn't retire until 1975, when he was the oldest active player at age 48.

✔ College basketball coaches were given permission to talk to their players during time outs.

Down and Dirty

A week after the NFL-AAFC announcement, the Philadelphia Eagles met the Los Angeles Rams in the NFL Championship Game. The Eagles had won the title the year before, thanks in part to the snowstorm that blanketed Philadelphia and favored their physical style of play (see page 82). The 1949 game, by contrast, was to be played in Los Angeles, where Rams quarterback Bob Waterfield and end Tom Fears were used to endless sunshine and big passing plays.

But the skies opened up on December 17, the day before the game, and three inches of rain fell by kickoff. It was the first time the Rams had played a home game in the rain since they moved west in 1946, and the field at the Los Angeles Memorial Coliseum was a sloppy mess.

Steve Van Buren again starred for Philadelphia, splashing for 196 rushing yards. End Pete Pihos caught a 31-yard touchdown pass from Tommy Thompson, Len Skladany scored after blocking Waterfield's punt, and the Eagles won the championship 14–0.

RESOURCES

1940s Events and Personalities

**Babe Didrikson Zaharias:
The Making of a Champion**
By Russell Freedman (New York:
Clarion Books, 1999)
*The most remarkable female athlete of
her time—and perhaps of any time—Babe
Didrikson Zaharias excelled at just about
any sport she tried.*

The Big Book of World War II
By Melissa Wagner and Dan Bryant
(Philadelphia: Running Press, 2009)
*A photo-packed book with stories about
World War II in Europe, Asia, and on the
American home front.*

Jackie Robinson
By Michael Teitelbaum (New York:
Sterling, 2009)
*A new biography of the baseball pioneer
aimed at middle-grade students.*

Satch and Me
By Bill Gutman (New York: Amistad,
2009)
*This novel imagines what it would be like
if a modern kid went back in history to
have adventures with the great pitcher
Satchel Paige.*

American Sports History

**The Encyclopedia of North American
Sports History, Second Edition**
Edited by Ralph Hickok (New York:
Facts On File, 2002)
*This title includes articles on the origins
of all the major sports as well as capsule
biographies of key figures.*

**Encyclopedia of Women and Sport
in America**
Edited by Carol Oglesby et al. (Phoenix:
Oryx Press, 1998)
*A large overview of not only key female
personalities on and off the playing field,
but a look at issues surrounding women
and sports.*

Encyclopedia of World Sport
Edited by David Levinson and Karen
Christensen (New York: Oxford
University Press, 1999)
*This wide-ranging book contains short
articles on an enormous variety of sports,
personalities, events, and issues, most of
which have some connection to American
sports history. This is a great starting
point for additional research.*

The ESPN Baseball Encyclopedia
Edited by Gary Gillette and Pete
Palmer (New York: Sterling, 2008, fifth
edition)
*This is the latest version of a long-running
baseball record and stats books, including
the career totals of every Major Leaguer.
Essays in the book cover baseball history,
team history, overviews of baseball in
other countries, and articles about the role
of women and minorities in the game.*

ESPN SportsCentury

Edited by Michael McCambridge (New York: Hyperion, 1999)

Created to commemorate the 20th century in sports, this book features essays by well-known sportswriters as well as commentary by popular ESPN broadcasters. Each decade's chapter features an in-depth story about the key event of that time period.

Facts and Dates of American Sports

By Gordon Carruth and Eugene Ehrlich (New York: Harper & Row, 1988)

Very detailed look at sports history, focusing on when events occurred. Large list of birth and death dates for major figures.

The Sporting News Chronicle of 20th Century Sports

By Ron Smith (New York: BDD/Mallard Press, 1992)

A good single-volume history of key sports events. They are presented as if written right after the event, thus giving the text a "you are there" feel.

Sports of the Times

By David Fischer and William Taafe (New York: Times Books, 2003)

A unique format tracks the top sports events on each day of the calendar year. Find out the biggest event for every day from January 1 to December 31.

Total Baseball

Edited by John Thorn, Pete Palmer, and Michael Gershman. (New York: Total Sports, 2004, eighth edition)

The indispensable bible of baseball, it contains the career records of every Major Leaguer. Essays in the front of the book cover baseball history, team history, overviews of baseball in other countries, and articles about the role of women and minorities in the game.

Sports History Web Sites

ESPN.com

www.sports.espn.go.com

The Web site run by the national cable sports channel contains numerous history sections within each sport.

Official League Web Sites

www.nfl.com
www.nba.com
www.mlb.com
www.nhl.com

Each of the major sports leagues has history sections on their official Web sites.

The Sporting News "Vault"

www.sportingnews.com/archives

More than 100 years old, The St. Louis-based Sporting News *is the nation's oldest sports weekly. In the history section of its Web site, it has gathered hundreds of articles on sports events, championships, stars, and more. It also includes audio clips of interviews with top names in sports from yesterday and today.*

Sports Reference

www.sports-reference.com

By far the most detailed central site, including separate sections on baseball, basketball, football, hockey, and the Olympics. The sections include player stats, team histories, records from all seasons past, and much more.

INDEX